TURNING POINTS IN WOMEN'S LIVES

From the 20th to the 21st Century

Nuevo
Books

Los Ranchos, NM

TURNING POINTS
IN
WOMEN'S LIVES

From the 20th to the 21st Century

To Ann,
To inspire your own
story.
Shirley Patterson Susan Cho

Shirley L. Patterson and Susan A. Cho, Editors

Nuevo Books
Los Ranchos, New Mexico
2012

© 2012, Nuevo Books

All rights reserved.
Nuevo Books
Los Ranchos, New Mexico
www.NuevoBooks.com

Printed in the U.S.A.

Book design by Paul Rhetts
Cover photograph by Shirley Patterson

Library of Congress Cataloging-in-Publication Data

Turning points in women's lives : from the 20th to the 21st century / Shirley L. Patterson and Susan A. Cho, editors.
p. cm.
ISBN 978-1-936745-06-7 (pbk. : alk. paper)
1. Older women--United States--Biography.
2. Women--United States--Biography.
3. Women--United States--Social conditions--20th century.
4. Women--United States--Social conditions--21st century.
5. Life change events--United States--Case studies.
6. Influence (Psychology)--Case studies.
7. United States--Biography.
8. Retired women--New Mexico--Albuquerque--Biography.
9. Albuquerque (N.M.)--Biography.
I. Patterson, Shirley Louise.
II. Cho, Susan A., 1943-
HQ1064.U5T88 2012
920.720973--dc23
2011053254

DEDICATED TO

the insightful women of La Vida Llena who shared with us significant moments in time that had lasting impact over decades of living – and to all women who follow similar, but different, turning points in their lives.

CONTENTS

ACKNOWLEDGMENTS

We wish to extend our appreciation to the Full Life Foundation and its President and Chairman of the Board, Bill Nordyke, for helping us launch this book by providing a "Book Signing" event at La Vida Llena. The Full Life Foundation is an independent nonprofit 501(c)(3) entity established to provide assistance to La Vida Llena residents who may experience financial difficulties at some point during their tenure. Profits from this book will be donated to the Full Life Foundation.

Our thanks...to Mari-Luci Jaramillo for her early encouragement in moving this book forward...to Linda Givens, Executive Director of La Vida Llena, for her continuing support of this project...to Ramona Caplan and Jane Koch, who assisted some authors by typing their stories into digital format...to Shirl Brainard for introducing us to Barbe Awalt of Nuevo Books...to Barbe Awalt for her publishing expertise and helpful suggestions...to Mary Ridgeway for proofing of the book.

The Editors

FOREWORD

"Turning Points in Women's Lives" is a welcome look at the lives of real women spanning much of the 20th century and continuing to the 21st. None of the authors are, or ever were, famous. None made history with new discoveries, public feats of daring, infamous acts of defiance, or spectacular inventions. But they invented lives worth living, and lives worth learning about.

When most of us meet a woman who is past a "certain age," we tend to view her as just an "old lady." She has always been the age she is now. But we are so wrong. We don't know how she looked, what she felt, what she feared, and what she accomplished at 20, 30, 40, 50, or beyond. This book gives us a glimpse of lives well lived, and events that shaped those lives.

"Turning Points..." is rich in diversity — diversity of its writers, diversity of their backgrounds and geography, and diversity in the way they approach life. A fascinating potpourri of real events and adventures, laced with memories good and bad, along with turning points that made life meaningful and rewarding. Some adversity yes — but much joy and incredible resilience.

Read this book. You will never again see "just an old lady" when you meet a woman long past the bloom of youth and the trials of middle age. You will meet a woman of substance, and ask yourself — "Where has she been, and what can I learn?"

Martha Burk, Ph.D.

Martha Burk is a women's rights advocate who is former Chair of the National Council of Women's Organizations. She is currently Money Editor for Ms. magazine, and has a syndicated column and radio show. She served as Senior Advisor for Women's Issues to Governor Bill Richardson of New Mexico, and is the author of *Politics Matters: What's At Stake for Women in 2012 and Beyond*. Her motto, "If I can't dance, I won't come to your revolution," comes from the early 20th century labor activist, Emma Goldman. She resides in Corrales, New Mexico with her husband, Ralph Estes.

INTRODUCTION

"Turning Points in Women's Lives" evolved out of a grassroots organization that became known as The Gathering of Women at La Vida Llena (LVL). Established in 1983, LVL is a life care retirement community in Albuquerque, New Mexico.

In the summer of 2008, a small planning committee of women residents met to develop a women's group that would meet particular wishes and needs of women to:

...be "issue" informed,

...experience inner growth and development,

...create a caring, supportive community and

...have fun.

Meetings would be held once a month (except for a break in July and August) and speakers would be selected alternately between noteworthy women in the larger community and women residents of La Vida Llena. The presentations centered on how each woman "moved" from "here to there" in her life. For instance, when the New Mexico Lieutenant Governor spoke, she entitled her presentation "My Pathway to the Lieutenant Governorship." Similarly when a resident spoke, she called her presentation, "The Many Hats I Have Worn."

Presentations by resident and community speakers included such pathways as working on legislative health care reform, moving out of an abusive marriage, becoming a country lawyer, challenges to a woman in academia, serving as a physician in the military and becoming a surgeon in a male dominated specialty.

The planning committee arranged a supportive environment for the presentations which included a light brunch, round table seating for ease of conversation, and individual printed invitations to all LVL women for each meeting. For the next three years these elements blended together to create a place where women's knowledge, emotions and enjoyment could meet and be shared.

This kind of experience led to a sense of kinship, empowerment and trust among the women. Sharing life stories had become very important. It was at this point that the editors thought more could be done with the interest engendered. Participants in The Gathering of Women might share their life stories through the written word.

Also, drawing on our professional social work backgrounds we understood the significance of reminiscence for people as they age. A psychiatrist, Robert Butler, postulated the psychological benefits of life review, or reminiscing, as people grow older. It is an activity that allows us to look back in our lives and make sense of life events and decisions made.

We developed guidelines for the project. The most important was a question to focus the stories: "**What person, event or group significantly influenced your life? How?**" The guidelines also included the length, time frame, and instructions for submitting the stories in digital format as required for editing and publication. In small group meetings we introduced the project, offered examples, and encouraged the women to talk about their story ideas.

When some women were not able to use a computer, volunteers typed hand-written stories onto their computers. A few women with vision and other limitations found someone to write down their story as they told it.

After we read, edited, made suggestions on each story, and discussed potential changes, the authors finalized their stories for publication. The editor-author process of discussing each story enriched the outcome for all of us.

We heard over and over from the authors that their process of deciding on a subject for their story and thinking through how it affected their lives was dynamic and produced feelings of wonder at what they had lived, accomplishment at having lived it, and satisfaction from producing a story that meant so much to them and could be shared — especially with their own families.

Of course, there have been many details to work out in getting this book published. But, by far the most extraordinary part of the process has been the experience of interacting with the courageous, perceptive, earnest women authors and their moving stories.

Shirley L. Patterson and Susan A. Cho, Editors

The "Boss" Lives On
by
Gee Arrom

When I was little, maybe 5 or 6 years of age, my older sister, Sally, was always mothering me. She was 14 years my senior and one of her phrases I heard over and over was, "Yes, you can do it. Just work a little harder." She constantly wanted me to be all the things she wanted to be, but never had time or a benefactor to help her along.

I was happy just being a child with all the good things in life to enjoy. The farm life I lived until I was 15 supplied me with sustenance, shelter, and siblings who spoiled me as I was the "baby" of the household.

While in grade school I kept changing my mind as to what I wanted to become when I grew up — one day it was a music teacher and the next an Army nurse or even a General. I loved playing dress up and was in all the school plays; so Hollywood was another option. I nixed that soon, because I never wanted to be so far from home. Then I thought the best thing would be to marry a man in town and have babies to spoil. That way I could stay close to Mom and Dad. Alas, that thought changed when I went through high school. All the while "the boss" was whispering in my ear, "Get out of the small town and see the world."

Strangely enough it happened. I was training for practical nursing and I had arranged work with some patients when WWII ended and I met the father of my children at a square dance. He had returned from serving in the Merchant Marines and said it was a "fluke" that he even came to that dance. But that's where our life together really began. We were smitten with each other and soon married in Oklahoma City where he was going to Air Traffic Control School.

From then on we lived in one place after another, including five of the other U.S. states. We ended up living in Spain, England, the Virgin Islands, and Alaska, where three of our five beautiful children were born. I have seen everything from elk, moose, bear and ptarmigan running through my yard. I've flown all over the frozen North in a small airplane. My life was exciting and busy. My oldest sister was amazed how quickly her idea of how "my life" should be, actually came to be.

My first experience in the early years of my marriage was moving to a remote station in Alaska with only six houses and a weather station to keep us posted on severe storms that might be heading our way. There was a small Army post not too far away and occasionally one of the guys would go off the deep end and meander into our midst. We women had to hang our wash in the basement because of the winds and severe cold. One day as we collected the wash, three of us found our under garments either missing or the bottoms cut out of them. Needless to say, when they caught that guy, he was "Sectioned 8," meaning he needed psychiatric help.

Our life amongst the brown bears in Kodiak was always more excitement than I needed. I had a two year old child then and it was a constant worry when he went out to play. I was ready to give up the life in the north, but my sister's words, "You can do it," always pervaded my thoughts and I would try harder to master the situation.

I was only 24 years old and all the other women were in their 30s. My life was harder because I didn't fit in very well. However, my practical nursing helped me be accepted. I offered my services to all who became ill, so they wouldn't have to make a trip into Anchorage.

The Civil Aeronautics Administration (CAA) — now called the Federal Aeronautics Administration (FAA) — provided plane service only twice a month to bring the mail. My husband bought a small plane on floats that could be converted to skis and that earned us great respect. Alaskan life was not easy. The weather, remote stations and constant mechanical problems with our aircraft were everyday occurrences. More than once, while flying along the beach area in southeastern Cordova, our engine quit and we had to land on a rocky beach; only to find the trouble was water in the gas – a fixable problem. Getting back in the air was "white-knuckle" time and I wanted to wait for a boat to come along. But Sally's "little" voice would float across my mind saying, "You can do it."

It has been that way most of my life. When she became ill in the '80s, I went to stay with her. When the end was near she told me, "Get your bags packed and leave." We both had tears dripping off our chins as we said our goodbyes. For once I played "boss" and whispered in her ear, "You can do it." A week later she passed to another place.

I still hear her "bossing" me whenever a situation arises that I can't seem to handle. Her voice has not only influenced my life, but has spread to two generations. I used her format to "boss" my brood the same way. Today I can hear my son saying to his children, "Get with it. You can do it." The "boss" lives on.

As Long as I Can Remember, I Wanted to Be a Mom
by
Phyllis Barnes

When I was 6 years old, our mother left us. Our father asked his mother, then 55 years old and living on a farm in Missouri, to come to Oregon to care for his two little girls. We lived in a remote farmhouse near a tiny little town. Our farmhouse had no electricity or running water. It had the proverbial wooden outhouse complete with a crescent moon on the creaky door.

Because we were very poor, we had no store-bought toys or books. After doing our chores each day, we'd use our imaginations to entertain ourselves. We had an orchard of plum trees and our favorite activity was climbing trees to sit on the branches and watch the animal-shaped clouds drift by, or playing hide-and-seek between the trees, or having barefoot races from one end of the orchard to the other. My sister always won!

Our grandmother made all our dresses — yes, girls didn't wear pants in those days — on a treadle sewing machine from flour sacks. One day she crumpled up into a ball a scrap leftover from one of our dresses, put another scrap over it, and tied a piece of yarn at the bottom of the ball. She sewed a couple of mismatched buttons on the ball and it immediately became my "baby."

My baby never left my side, except when I went to school. She went with me when I gathered the eggs each morning; she was in my pocket when I milked Bossie each morning and evening; she sat on the table and watched while I took my weekly sponge bath, using the enamel pan that held water that had been warmed on the wood stove. She was with me whenever I was invited to the Joiner farm next door to play with my best friend, Kathleen. And, of course, baby slept with me every night in the bed I shared with my sister. She loved me unconditionally.

When I was 12 years old, my father remarried. My new stepmother lived in the big city of Eugene in a house that had electricity, running water, a flush toilet, a sink with water faucets, and even a telephone. As we unpacked all our belongings at the new house, our stepmother spied an old, never-washed rag, on the top of my box of belongings. She immediately grabbed it and held it by her finger tips as far away from her body as she could. She said she didn't know why on earth I had brought that rag along to our beautiful new house. She marched out to the garbage can, tossed it in, and slammed the lid shut. I followed her all the way, crying and pleading with her, trying to explain to her about baby. But she refused to listen and forbade me to retrieve it from the garbage.

When I was 22 years old, I married and was looking forward to becoming a mother. When I was 28, my doctor called to make an appointment for me and my husband to meet with him. Because I had several miscarriages, he recommended that we consider adoption. I was immediately taken with the idea; my husband said he was unwilling to raise a child that wasn't his own. But after several months, he relented.

Two different friends had given us baby showers, and I had spent months transforming our extra bedroom into a yellow and aqua paradise with a zoo of stuffed animals. On April 13, 1965, we received a telephone call from the Washington Children's Home

Society to ask if we were available to come to Yakima the next day at 1:00 pm. There was someone they wanted us to meet. OF COURSE WE WERE AVAILABLE!

I finally met our baby — a three-month-old little (not so little - 15 lbs.!) boy. He was completely bald on the top of his head, but had a circle of red hair around his head. He looked like a little monk. His eyes were bright blue and he had perfect little hands and feet! They placed him into my waiting arms. After walking around the room and talking with him for several minutes, I knew he was the one I had been waiting for, for so long. We were allowed to take him home. I was finally a mom.

There had been such emptiness to my life before my son came to us. I had tried to fill that emptiness with being the best wife I could be, with a job, with volunteer activities, with church work. But there was such a longing; it actually physically hurt at times. Giving a mother's love and receiving that love in return from my child was my heart's fulfillment.

Even now that I'm an old granny, any time I spend with young ones gives me such delight! A special place in my heart has been filled by my children and grandchildren. They have made ALL the difference in my life.

P.S. Ron is now 46 years old, the father of my two grandchildren — the joy of my life! Two years after Ron's adoption, we had our own biological daughter, and 10 years later we had another daughter. You never know what the Lord has planned for you!

Father and the Eternal Wallflower

by
Elizabeth Shellabarger Bayne

It seemed a long time coming. As a junior in high school I was going to run for Student Council Secretary, had been selected to be in the elite choir, and almost felt like a "person," vis-à-vis the eternal wallflower.

Then my father, a Navy officer, came home and announced the family was going to move — AGAIN. This had happened before, but this was just before my senior year. I was devastated. How could this be happening? My life was in ruins!

Try as I might to explore and present every possibility of remaining in Norfolk, Virginia, the response was always a stern, "You will go with the family." And where were we going? To Bogotá, Colombia — all the way to South America. Good grief, not only was my life in ruins, I'd be lost forever!

That was the summer of 1955. I was barely 15 and my life was over, or so I thought.

My father was no ogre, just smart, and certainly knew what was best for his eldest daughter. He was also loving, kind, handsome and the fairest person I have ever known. I knew that, but right then it didn't matter much. Being a teenager kicked in and I behaved miserably for a while.

Well, we moved that summer — to Washington, DC — to a three-bedroom apartment and it was HOT. I had three younger sisters and there was only one air-conditioned room in that apartment – my parents' bedroom. We would put the little girls in that room until they fell asleep and then move them to their room. My other sister, Susan and I would take over the cool room to settle down and relax, and then move to our room. Then Mother and Daddy would get some rest.

That summer Mother took Spanish lessons — an adventure. She had studied French in school and was very creative. She devised a wonderful mix of English, French and Spanish which truly endeared her with her newfound Colombian friends in the years to come. I had taken Spanish for four years in high school and my father spoke it rather well. We three practiced a lot that summer.

Also that summer I took driving lessons, which was quite an adventure in the big city. There were so many sights to drive to — monuments and statues and beautiful buildings. I even learned to negotiate traffic circles. The payoff was driving with my father from Washington, DC, to New York City. We were taking the car — a huge pale green Chrysler -- to the dock where it could be loaded on the ship that would take us to South America. But there was a dock strike and we could not leave the car at the assigned place for fear of vandalism. I do not recall how Daddy solved this dilemma. But he did, and we took the train back to Washington, DC.

Yes, we were going by ship, a Grace Lines ship, the Santa Paula. Things were looking up! Daddy had declared he was not packing any crinoline petticoats. So sister Sue and I wore every one we were taking. I had three and one was red tulle. What a sight we were — we looked like toy tops. When we left New York City we ran straight into a hurricane. Susan and I spent the better part of two days lashed to our deck chairs riding out stormy seas. The third morning was calm again and it was like we had stopped in port overnight and taken on new passengers — lots of new faces and people everywhere.

We docked in Cartegena, a completely new world. I was hearing Spanish and beginning to think in Spanish. I became the family translator. There were poinsettia trees taller than I was and coffee trees! All our worldly goods were off-loaded and began their journey by river boat and cartage to the capital city, Bogotá, which lies at 9,000 feet in a large verdant valley.

Father determined we would not live in the English-speaking community. After about six weeks in an apartment we moved into a three bedroom home, fairly close to downtown. The owners lived in an apartment at street level and our home was the entire second floor. It was entered by going up a grand, broad, stone staircase with elegant wrought iron railings. Also on the street level was the garage and behind that the servants' quarters. Yes, we had two "live-ins" and a laundress who came once a week. Daddy had a chauffeur and an official car. There was also a small back patio with broken glass embedded in the top of the walls — to discourage the "ladrones," or thieves, we were told. This house was on a hill at the base of the foothills. The street was about two blocks long. At the bottom was a nice city park. The bus ran along that main street.

You may recall, I had completed my junior year of high school. In Bogotá there was a German school, the American school (Colegio Nueva Granada) and, of course, Colombian schools. However, the American school only went through the 9th grade at that time. I never actually graduated from high school. I took Algebra, English and Social Studies correspondence courses through the University of Nebraska Extension Division. My monitors were my father and the principal of Colegio Nueva Granada, Dr. Bjork.

There is something I have neglected to mention in this story. I began taking piano lessons when I was 5 years old. Music is what I know best and I felt confident and competent in that realm. Guess what? Colegio Nueva Granada needed a music teacher; so at age

15½, I began teaching school. Two of my sisters were my students. I taught music to all the grades and developed a school choir. We put on a variety show and gave two concerts a year. We were even invited the second year to sing at the American Embassy Christmas gala. That was an honor and my parents were proud of me. I was only 17 years old.

Colombia is a beautiful country, close to the equator and thus tropical. At 9,000 feet Bogotá had a mild climate, which was never too hot or cold. As a family we took many road trips, interesting and rudimentary roads though they were. Daddy loved to go to the farmers' markets and buy one of every piece of fruit or vegetable he saw. We would take them home and have grand "tastings" in the kitchen. One fruit I particularly remember was a gnarly round item, about the size of an apple, but with flesh the color of a beet and peppered with minute black seeds like a kiwi. It had soft flesh and a sweet mild taste. I never knew its name.

In 1957 there was a revolution. The dictator, General Gustavo Rojas Pinilla, was deposed from the presidency by other leaders. There was no major fighting, but there were incidents. Susan, always curious, heard a commotion one weekend day and went down near the park at the bottom of the hill. There was much chanting and shouting and then the police and soldiers arrived — whoosh — there were many people running up our street. Daddy was on the front steps and rapidly counted us girls, "One, two, three, four," and shut the door when we were inside. However, there on the steps looking up at him was a boy about 8 years old, quaking and asking for safety. Daddy sort of tucked him behind his body, next to the wall, and watched the authorities pass by. I am sure that youngster has always remembered the tall American who may have saved him that day.

Many of our friends did not know where their fathers were for some days — they had been arrested by Pinilla's guards and were detained in the bullring. But all returned home safely.

Naval officers are reassigned regularly (I was in 13 different schools before I entered the fourth grade) and Daddy's tour of duty would be completed at the end of 1957 when I was college bound. Since Daddy was a native of Colorado and there was a music school at the University of Colorado, the decision was made. I took no ACTs or SATs, but was registered at the University of Colorado.

Susan had completed the 9th grade and our parents decided the two of us would return to the United States together. I was 17 and she was 14. She would go to Utah to live with an aunt and uncle for a semester and I to the University of Colorado.

How would we get there? On a banana boat, of course! Our family flew in the military plane to Panama and, in the most torrential rain, Susan and I bid adios to our parents and two younger sisters. Our steamer trunks were loaded onto a small launch; we boarded and went off in the downpour. Everything and everyone we knew and loved were soon out of sight.

In front of us loomed a ship — another Grace Lines— and it was a freighter, not a cruise ship. Up went our trunks on a hoist and we climbed a rope ladder. A new journey began.

I have always wondered what if I had convinced my father to let me stay in Norfolk and graduate from high school in December of 1955, at the age of 15. Where might I have attended college? Would I have gone to Colombia at all? Would I have become a music teacher? Would I have been the eternal wallflower?

This event was the first of many when decisions were made, this one by my father. Since then I have made many decisions by myself. I am so glad I had a smart, loving, kind, handsome and FOREVER FAIR father. His considerations have always been and will continue to be part of decisions I make.

Georgia O'Keeffe & Me
by
Shirl Brainard

I suppose you might think it's perfectly audacious of me to say that Georgia O'Keeffe was a person of great influence in my life. She didn't know me from Adam, as the saying goes. I didn't know her either, but I knew *about her!*

My first year of college was at a small "junior" (community) college outside of Boston, Massachusetts. I was an art major and on a field trip to The Boston Museum of Art, I saw my first original O'Keeffe painting. It was her *Red Poppy.* I also saw my first Alexander Calder mobile and those two are all that I remember.

However, it wasn't until I had been through two divorces and was a single mother of a son in middle school, that Georgia entered my life. I was an Administrative Assistant to the Art Program Director and teaching a Drawing class at a Community College in Michigan. More and more of O'Keeffe's work appeared in art periodicals. By this time the poppy painting loomed large in my memory. It was a *huge* painting. But I still thought of her only as an artist, a *PAINTER*, not as a real *living* human person. She was distant — almost unreal, like all of the other celebrated artists I knew or recognized by studying or reading about their artwork. Oh, those *psychotic* artists such as Van Gogh or Gauguin who had led unusual *Bohemian-Arty-Life-Styles, everyone knew about them!*

Evan, my son, gifted me with the first book published with O'Keeffe's paintings, Christmas 1977. I was smitten with her art. She was my hero.

Joining the Navy after high school graduation, my son ended up in San Diego. My mother and I visited him there and went on to explore southern California. At the La Jolla Museum of Contemporary Art, Mom bought for me, *Portrait of an Artist, A Biography of Georgia O'Keeffe,* by Laurie Lisle.

Coming from a family of strong-willed women, no wonder Georgia appealed to me, and Mom also. The Great Depression had left my mom a single mother and my grandmother the strong matriarch that kept us going. Mom already had earned her small rural town's wrath for going to college – getting a divorce and later buying a car! In that town women didn't do those things!

It's interesting how society labels one: Doctor, Teacher, Mother, Wife, or Professor-Artist. These titles describe what these people do, not their characters. When we visited California, I was just beginning to know my mother as a *person* – not just *my MOTHER*. I don't know how Mom knew about Georgia, but they were of the same generation, there being only 17 years between them. No doubt she told me and I don't remember, but we discussed Georgia frequently.

I was having problems with my own identity. I didn't know for sure what I wanted for myself, where I wanted to go or how to get there.

While reading the book, Georgia became my mentor, *unknown* to her. As I read how she made decisions about *her life,* I think I heard her giving me permission to begin pursuing what I wanted to *do.* What I learned from Georgia was how to prioritize my own personal needs — and relationships. Some of Georgia's words

16

made me realize I no longer needed or wanted a man in my life, as husband *or* lover. I had no time (except for my son who was now grown and on the path of his own life). And I learned to say NO to social invitations I had no interest in. I said a big YES to things I wanted to do or pursue.

I made a list of goals. O'Keeffe's words, "Form, color and pattern are more important than subject," and her, "Filling a space in a beautiful way," made me understand that I wanted to further my own education in Design and Color Theory. It was easy for me to study alone and be my own companion. As an only child, I'd learned early to amuse myself by drawing, coloring, cutting, pasting and reading…(those still play important roles in my life).

It was easy for me to adapt her strategy: "… must use one's energy for their work." She spoke of her mind: "… as a plot of earth"… and, "the demands of my plot are relentless if anything is to grow in it… and must be tended with care, by myself." Her words became my mantra. More books began to be published about this *loner-woman* painter, and the more I devoured her words, the more I admired her self-sufficiency and self control.

I read that often she was considered cold, formidable, and difficult. That she was rude and didn't like people. However, I also read that she was a *good friend* to her friends, and did indeed like the company of people *IF* they had something to say or discuss. She chose her friends with care and kept them for many years.

Another thing I learned was about her sense of humor. Much later an Abiquiu resident, who worked for Georgia, told me that outside her house was a big stone slab where she had a collection of smaller stones. While working in her yard, he would move one stone. Maybe the next day he'd find it moved a bit another way and he'd move it again. Neither ever mentioned this quiet "game."

Through Georgia's unknown and absent guidance as my *Muse*, I studied and learned – and I practiced what I learned by painting or making collages. This self-education process concurred with my added teaching of Design and Color in the art program at the college.

And then Georgia died! When the 1986 Summer-term ended, I felt obliged to go to New Mexico and see where she'd lived and painted. Mom and I arrived in Albuquerque on a hot day in August. Driving north, the new scenery was thrilling. We drove straight to Abiquiu, turned at Bode's General Store, drove up the hill and arrived in front of Georgia's house — only to have a security guard tell us to "move on." That trip later brought both Mom and me to New Mexico to live. I felt Georgia had invited us!

A funny thing happened after Georgia's death. That next year I took a group of art students to the Chicago Art Institute to see a Retrospective show of O'Keeffe's. I saw again the *Red Poppy* and was shocked to see it was SO SMALL: 7 by 9 inches! Had I mentally morphed the painting's size to the woman's character and personality?

Georgia O'Keeffe suffered several emotional depressions that left her bereft and frightened. I too have gone through similar periods and know, if it weren't for my art, I wouldn't have survived.

I have never had illusions about becoming a famous painter myself. My creativity is limited, but the intensity I have, and my dedication to design and color, has led me to contribute what skills and knowledge I have to others. I transferred and shared my design and color information by writing a college textbook. That book has survived on the publisher's market for twenty years, being revised three times and translated into Chinese for sale in China.

The first years living in New Mexico, I facilitated *Artists' Retreats* at Ghost Ranch, a Presbyterian Learning Center. Located on the same acreage was one of Georgia's two homes. We met as a group of painters to try and interpret the area's fabulous colors and earth structures into paintings. The first year we all noticed that a single black crow appeared *everywhere* we went. I wrote the following:

The Crow

Whoosh … whoosh … whoosh!
With a flap of her wings, I heard her caw.
I knew it was HER!
As always, dressed in black, she watched as she circled round
       and round –
Watching. Forever watching us as we tried to grasp the essence of
her hills, her sky, her space – even *her* mountain.
I put her in my drawing.
I captured her new form.
She seemed appeased.
Did she think I'd forgotten her?

Thank you, Georgia, for your inspiration and support. You may
have spoken through my Mom. Only you two will ever know.

Turn Around

by
Patricia Risley Campbell

I grew up in a traditional, church-going, sheltered family. The expectations were to behave, know how to help at home, do well in school, not to ever upset the man of the family and always work toward his comfort. We were active in church, learned household skills, enjoyed each other, learned music, read books. I excelled in academic work, but was definitely lacking in self-esteem and how to socialize with boys. Like many young women in the late forties and the fifties, I bought the general beliefs of that time: that we should, if possible, get a college education for a marketable skill, but in any case marry, help a husband through his education, have at least four children, and keep a well-run home. That was to be our primary task. Magazines and the media in general brought us examples of the good housewife: how to cook, sew, raise children correctly and manage the home for the husband.

I found myself with a high honors college education, marriage, a job, putting my husband through his M.A. degree and being criticized harshly by him every day. I wasn't good enough. Four children came along and we had a small home in the suburbs. I was increasingly depressed, and even tried several times to run away. I became dependent and put myself in a victim role. Then came the events that totally changed my life.

My husband came home one day and told me he wanted to become an educational missionary. This news thrilled me as that had always been my dream. He began to try to change, to become more sensitive to people and to become closer to his family during the long application and selection process. We finally were accepted and began six months of training. Those were the happiest times of our marriage.

We trained in a community of other applicants. The children were cared for all day, spouses were in separate discussion groups, and I began to be respected for my thinking and expression of opinions. There was no criticism of me when I talked. In contrast, in my home I was to keep quiet, not to express opinions in front of others. Then we moved to the language school (Spanish) in Costa Rica where, again, I could revel in learning and discussion. There was help in the home, the children were rapidly learning in local schools and we were happier as a couple when we worked for a common goal.

The move to Peru was harder; life there was much more difficult. I again had help in the home and began teaching in a school where my children were students. They adapted quite well and quickly formed friendships — they were the only North American children in that city, several miles from Lima. We had all had to change countries, language, culture, living style, and, with the military coup during our first year, to live under a dictatorship.

Increasingly I became more independent, leaning less on my husband, especially as he began to lash out at his family and became more reclusive with the stress of all the changes. I began to see the United States from a different viewpoint which upset him greatly. Whereas I had been fortunate to grow up in a family with a broad world view, he had grown up in a narrow way of thinking with much less acceptance of differences. He was appalled that I would criticize the United States, ordered me to think just the way he did, and tried to forbid me to speak critically of U.S. policy.

We were touched by the news of the upheaval of the Vietnam War, the Civil Rights Movement, and then the Women's Movement. I was excited by the latter when, in my own thinking, I had begun to criticize what I had allowed at home. Reading that others in the U.S. were writing in the same vein brought me to realize that I had compromised my own integrity by allowing myself to be abused and put down almost continually. It was a huge blow.

In addition to all of this, on May 30, 1970, there was a tragically huge earthquake in Peru, some miles north of our home. I had been in the mountains with a friend and was riding home on a dirt road down from the 16,000 foot pass. We jolted over rocks, more and more debris, and finally were stopped by a huge landslide many miles from Lima. It grew darker; we heard dimly on the radio about the destruction on the coast. I crawled in the dark over the slide to find transportation on the other side. In Lima I found a bus to take me home. I was shaken, cut, filthy, but found the children were all right.

In the aftermath, still shaking for weeks and months, I began to reassess my situation, especially when I heard that my husband, as usual, was involved with a young woman while helping in the quake zone high in the mountains. The question I asked myself was: Do I want to live this way for the next fifty years? I wrote a letter to my supervisor in New York stating that I could no longer live with my husband, that I was afraid and repulsed, yet I wanted to remain in Peru.

The answering letter was blunt: I must return with the children to the United States and was to work at a mission school which I had never heard of in a small town in New Mexico. Within a few days after returning to the U.S., I obtained legal protection, got a driver's license and opened a bank account. The children began school (in English now) and I began to work. We had come over-night from Lima, and only had what was in our suitcases. It was a traumatic time for me as I was still shaking for almost a year, but I gained confidence, sense of self-esteem and independence. I was hostile and afraid to trust anyone; but, with time, that passed.

It took a change of country, language, culture, an earthquake and marital breakup; but, hardheaded as I am, it all brought me to where I am today. My children gained immeasurably because of their bilingualism and experiences in another culture. All went to college and two use Spanish daily in their professions. I remain self-confident, married to a man who respects me and what I can do, a man with a world view sensitive to social problems, and who has actively tried to make a difference. I am retired from a success-ful profession as a bilingual teacher, and am content and occupied in teaching seniors, activities in a retirement facility, and learning new skills.

My Children's Gift
by
Louise Chambellan

This is the story of my education and the very special event that led to my completing a college degree.

Navajo education developed slowly. In the treaty of 1868 the U.S. government promised a teacher and a school for every 30 children. Though this never actually came about, in the last few years the government has seen to it that a decent education is available to almost all Navajo children.

When I started going to school, before World War II, less than half of the Navajo children in school went to government boarding schools. A few went to Mission schools that were also boarding schools.

My education started at Saint Michael's Mission, a boarding school near Fort Defiance, Arizona. It was one of the first schools on the reservation. Many Indians have gone to Mission schools, probably because they are conveniently near their homes or because they had the reputation for being stricter. In those days, many children had to be forced to go to boarding school and often ran away. Nobody had to force me, because I wanted to go to school and see other children. I went to Saint Michael's for two years and then changed to the government boarding school at Fort Defiance, Arizona. I'm not sure why I changed, but perhaps because it was closer to my home and was bigger.

I stayed at Fort Defiance Boarding School until I graduated eighth grade. I remember some special teachers. My first grade teacher would have us lie down on blankets after recess and read us stories. She changed her voice for different characters. She wrote to me after she left Fort Defiance. My fifth grade teacher started Girl Scouts. My seventh and eighth grade teacher, a man, taught chorus and drama. That's where I learned how to sing.

After graduation from eighth grade, my sister, a cousin and I went to Ute Vocational School at Ignacio, Colorado. The Ute School was for Ute children, but some Navajo were allowed to go there. The two tribes had a history of warfare and had language and cultural differences. Sometimes we did not care for each other. There was not too much real friction; it was more a case of staying in our own group.

I liked school at Ignacio better than Fort Defiance. We had a better living situation: at Ignacio we had two girls to a room; whereas, at Fort Defiance we slept in a dormitory. We also could do our own laundry at Ignacio; at Fort Defiance our laundry was sent out and came back like a stiff board. At the Ute School the teachers were more interested in us and in doing a good job and there were lots of interesting things to learn. During the morning the girls had Home Economics and the boys had Agriculture. In the afternoons we had academic subjects.

After I graduated from high school, I married, worked a short time at the Ute School dining room and then started college at Old Fort Lewis in Hesperus, Colorado. I completed two years of college and then moved to Dulce, New Mexico, where my husband was teaching. My oldest son was born soon after and I stayed home to take care of him.

For the next several years we moved about every two years as my husband had different teaching jobs. I often helped my husband by visiting the students' parents and interpreting for him. I thought to myself: "Someday I want to be a teacher."

When we moved to Zuni, New Mexico, it was a miracle for me! There were more people around and I enjoyed the activity in Zuni Village. One day the principle of the Zuni School called my husband and asked if I would like to teach first grade. I answered, "Yes!" I found an excellent baby sitter and was really excited to teach first grade. I was also scared, because I had never been around a group of children. The principle showed me where my classroom was, showed me the lesson plan and the books we'd use for reading, math and spelling. She introduced me to the class – and I was on my own. I soon got used to teaching and knew what to do.

I did not have a degree. The Bureau of Indian Affairs (BIA) schools could hire you without a degree if you were Indian. I taught second graders at Zuni for two years until the BIA school was closed and the children were sent to Gallup McKinley County school. All the BIA schools were eventually closed in favor of sending Indian children to regular public schools. I am glad I taught the Zuni students. After that I wanted to go back to college, but could not because I had four boys at home to take care of.

The principle of the Church Rock public school hired me to be a Librarian Aide and I learned how to arrange books and schedule classes to come to the Library. I read stories to kindergarten, first and second graders. I read the stories like my first grade teacher – with different voices for the characters. Later I became a Reading Aide.

Then we moved to Gallup, New Mexico, where my husband taught at Fort Wingate. I began to substitute teach at the local schools and had some good experiences with students. I liked what I was doing. After a time my husband was hired to be the principle at Tse Bonito Elementary School. He wanted me to transfer to Tse Bonito School, too. I told him, "I do not want to be transferred." But he told me he needed me to be an interpreter. It was nice and I learned how to interpret — English to Navajo and Navajo to English. I was also a Teaching Aide there for a year.

I now had five sons, all going to school in Gallup — two in high school, one in junior high school and two in elementary school. I was working as a Teacher Aide and also taking care of the house and the boys.

One day when my husband and I came home my sons had supper ready and we sat down at the table. My sons kept looking at each other. I guess they were trying to decide who was going to speak. They selected Curtis to speak. He said, "We all have decided that Mother should go back to college and get her degree. My brothers and I will take care of the house and Dad can take care of us." I was delighted — I could finally get my degree and be a real teacher. My children's gift made all the difference!

I went back to college at Fort Lewis in Durango, Colorado, and did my student teaching in Farmington, New Mexico. I graduated in 1975. Then, I began teaching second grade at Tse Bonito School. My husband retired and we had a new principle at Tse Bonito School. Sometimes he came to my classroom to talk about school and sometimes he came for advice.

A new school was being opened in the spring. The principle sent a message to the parents asking their help to name the school. He later came to my classroom and asked me if I had a name for the school. I said, "No." He said he didn't like the names the parents came up with – Burned Corn, Tse Bonito Springs, etc. I then mentioned some names and places, including Chee Dodge who was the first Chairman of the Navajo tribe. I went on to name some more names. He added Chee Dodge to the list. The next morning, the principle came to my room and said, "They named the new school Chee Dodge."

We all moved to the new school, Chee Dodge Elementary School. It was a nice school building with plenty of rooms. I taught there for two years and retired. Later I substituted there for a year and then we moved to Rio Rancho, New Mexico.

My five boys all went to college. I am glad for them. I am glad they made it possible for me to go back to college and get my degree.

Music: Food for My Soul
by
Lillian Chavez

"Striving for excellence" played a big part, not only in the way I approached music, but also the way I approached life. As I grew up in my family this life style was not verbalized — it was learned by example. So, it was only natural that when I was of an age (8 years old) to think about musical training, the teacher who was chosen would have the same values as my family.

A woman, whose name was Mrs. Echols, was chosen and I must say, she certainly set the tone for how I would study and prepare music lessons throughout my life. She was actually a "task master" — no fooling around and no fudging by moving the hands of the clock forward while practicing. She insisted on ONE FULL HOUR OF PRACTICE every day. If the fingering or rhythm was not correct during my lesson, out came the ruler and WHACK across my knuckles. (The effect of the ruler on my knuckles did not appear until I was 92.) I must say I was a fast learner because I didn't receive too many of those knuckle busters after my first encounter with the ruler. I suppose in today's society she would have been thrown in prison for her "ruler discipline," never to be heard from again. She was very much into, "if you are going to do something, do it right." This isn't all bad, but a bit wearing for an 8 year old not only to comprehend, but appreciate. However, she was an excellent teacher and when I received a compliment, believe me, it was well earned. I studied with her for ten years until I left the family home.

My love for the piano was pretty much put to rest for a number of years while I did my "thing" – two marriages (one a failure and one a success), two children and just living. Finally when my children were ready for musical training we bought a Baldwin Acrosonic piano. What a joy! After going through several teachers, we finally found a good one and I was very impressed with her method of teaching. I decided that not only would my youngest child be her pupil, but that I would also take lessons from her. This was a good decision. She gave me a tremendous amount of encouragement because after all it had been about 15 years since I had done any serious playing. Her actions and words renewed my faith in my abilities as a pianist. For several years she worked with me doing solo piano, but occasionally we would work up a one piano four hand duet and perform these pieces at little recitals held in her home. Since she had two grand pianos in her studio, she suggested that we start doing two piano four hand duets. One piano four hand music is great, but two piano four hand music is an orchestra! These are such a fun challenge. I was hooked!

Without her encouragement, not only in playing the piano, but her confidence in me that I would make a good piano teacher, I probably would not still be performing just for the joy of sharing the music. Thank you, Frances, for making me realize I can make beautiful music and am actually a decent musician.

Playing the piano over the years in a variety of settings has been very satisfying and rewarding. I had good teachers and some not so good. From each, however, I have come away having learned something. I am once again studying with a wonderful teacher who is a marvelous musician and half my age. We are having a grand time performing duets for both one piano and two pianos.

Excellence has played a significant role in my life, but music is food for my soul.

An Ending That Was a Beginning
by
Susan A. Cho

"Your Joy is your Sorrow unmasked. And the selfsame well from which your laughter raises was oftentimes filled with your tears."
from *The Prophet* by Khalil Gibran (1923).

While mulling over what to write about that has significantly influenced my own life, I cannot get past six and a half weeks of the life of my only child, Heidi Yukiko Cho. Those six and a half life-changing weeks were "life in a crucible" and, as it turned out, a practice run for facing what comes in life and moving forward.

Heidi was born on February 22 and died April 7, 1971. I was 27 years old. Tetsuo Cho, whom I met when we were both students at the University of California, Berkeley, had been my husband almost five years. Our life had been on track. I'd just completed a master's degree in Social Work and we were choosing to begin a family. Our marriage was based on shared values and ideals, though our personalities clashed at times with disagreements that rankled. My pregnancy and Heidi's delivery were uneventful. But, she was what in those days was called a "blue baby." The official diagnosis was "transposition of the major vessels," a very serious congenital heart defect.

I spent nights and days at the hospital, quickly learning the ways of a medical institution and facing my fear of hospitals. That fear stemmed from an experience when I was 5 and my father was in a terrible auto accident. My grandfather sneaked me into the hospital to see my father and I became weak and dizzy. Since that time I had never been comfortable in hospitals and, when it had been suggested to me, I wouldn't even consider becoming a nurse.

Having just completed my graduate degree in Social Work, I was also quite self-reflective through this traumatic experience. I found myself devastated, angry, hopeless and hopeful, as I struggled with my intense feelings. Tetsuo and I received support, love and company from my mother, brother and friends. We also suffered each other's inabilities to fully understand and meet each other's needs. There was an "emotional blow-up" when my mother criticized Tetsuo for not being nurturing enough with me and he retaliated with an angry critique of her husband. We also experienced the worry and anticipation of a burden of medical bills on our future income. We struggled with our fears of a life with a chronically ill child or life without our child. I suffered much angst over whether I was or could be a "good enough mother." Then it was over. Heidi was dead.

But our life remained. The week following Heidi's death I wrote what I called a "chronicle of our days with Heidi." In closing I stated, "I think it was good for me to think through the events again — perhaps I can now begin to forget them." Of course it was only the beginning of a process of grief that has never been forgotten or ever ended. Having and losing Heidi was a very rocky spot in my life path and it precipitated huge changes.

Loving Heidi showed me how deep, intense and powerful my feelings can be and gave me a glimmer of my ability to love and nurture.

Coping with and coming to terms with this first major loss

at age 27 was a practice for many losses to follow: my brother's accidental death at age 45, my father's death, my mother's death, the deaths of other family, friends, colleagues and clients that only become more numerous as I age. I have practiced valuing life, letting it go, and honoring it when it is gone.

My personal struggles with grief and loss and the enormity of all the interpersonal dynamics those struggles generated have enabled me to empathize with, be insightful about and, I think most of all, *patient* with my many social work clients over the years. Each of them came to me to work through something that in the end often related to processing a personal loss and trauma.

What I learned during the long days and nights at the hospital with Heidi also helped me overcome my childhood fear of hospitals and helped me gain the confidence to accept a social work job in a hospital. That job opened the door for several career moves in medical settings throughout my professional social work life.

As is not uncommon with couples who lose a child, my marriage did not survive the trauma. Tetsuo and I were divorced 16 months after Heidi died. I was not aware, at that relatively immature stage of life, how significant it is that men and women grieve differently or how those differences can be experienced as ignoring the other's needs. Any roots of incompatibility can be magnified by each partner's inability to meet the needs of the other while grieving. Even though no longer being married expanded my experience of loss, it also allowed me to explore and live a lifestyle that has been engaging, satisfying and deeply rewarding.

Losing my child robbed me of being a parent. But I have struggled, only in different contexts, through similar joys of pride and love, and fears of inadequacy and failure that I had anticipated in parenthood. I also had to, and did, find the rewards and benefits of life without children.

Each person's first experience with a significant loss is life changing. Mine came early, at age 27. By the grace of whatever gives my life momentum, I was not defeated by the loss. I was able to survive it, grow through it, and weave it into the fabric of my being where, to this day, it deepens my responses and understanding.

Army Life – Army Wife
by
Barbara Clark

I lived in Kansas City all my life until I went away to college. I had a protected childhood. My dad was a surgeon and a very strict parent. I mean strict: "Where are you going? When will you be back? How long have you known him? Who are his parents?" Very controlling. The Midwest was my world — a comfortable and nurturing world. I went to college at the University of Kansas, in Law-rence, Kansas, 30 miles away from my home. I majored in Political Science and minored in Spanish. However, I never planned to work; but wanted to be a credit to my husband.

I met Tom and never suspected that it was the beginning of a whole new world for me. He was in the V-12, a Navy program, and soon was off to the United States Military Academy, West Point, New York. While he was at West Point I saw him many times and we fell madly in love. For my junior year in college I applied to enter Vassar College in Poughkeepsie, New York, so I could be closer (25 miles away) to Tom at West Point. I was accepted, but when I arrived at my new dorm, I was WAY out of my element. This was not me. My wool skirt and sweater set worn with bobby socks and saddle shoes just did not mix with the "sloppy" sophistication (?) of the Vassar girls. I went home before even attending a class. Tom and I continued our long distance romance and became engaged. In June 1948, six days after Tom graduated from West Point, we hurried home to Kansas City for a big wedding and the rest of my life.

We were stationed two places over the summer while we awaited orders to go to Germany. However, Tom and three other classmates were selected to work in the atomic weapons special project at Sandia Base in Albuquerque, New Mexico. New Mexico was not like anything I'd ever seen — brown, sand, and dust storms.

As Tom made his way through the military ranks, I made my way through the ranks of the social circle of the officers' wives. When Tom was made Aide-de-Camp to the Post Commander, it was my job to be aide to the Post Commander's wife and help her with all manner of social events and activities she organized for the officers' wives. I was not in Kansas anymore. I was in a new society with many protocols, expectations and rules to learn. It also was a community where you never feel like a stranger. I was becoming an Army wife and I loved it.

This was the period following Hiroshima. Sandia Base was closely connected to Los Alamos which we knew did "secret things." Tom never came home saying, "Guess what happened today?" It was all top secret, but I knew important things happened at Los Alamos. The base grapevine gossiped about bombs being stored in the mountains.

Meanwhile my life as an Army wife was evolving. A general visiting from Washington, DC, had to stay on base longer than he planned. He needed a clean white shirt and I, ever wanting to be the helpful general's aide's wife, offered to wash his shirt despite the fact that I had never washed and ironed a shirt. Tom's shirts were always sent to the laundry. I washed, starched and ironed that shirt and took special care to make the front perfect. I was very proud of my accomplishment. I astonished my community of wives by speaking casually with the General as an equal — and learned another of many lessons in military protocol: no matter the context, a General is a General and not to be addressed casually. We used calling cards when visiting other officers. I left one card because I called on the wife; Tom left two cards because he called on the General and the wife.

Life marched on. Our family grew by three babies. Tom was sent to war in Korea. I returned to Kansas City so my parents could help me with the babies.

Communication to the war front was difficult. Unbeknownst to me, Tom was wounded and sent to Japan for care. A telephone operator called to tell me that Tom was going to call me at a certain time. We had not spoken in nearly a year (no cell phone, no SKYPE). I was nervous and excited. But when we were on the telephone we could barely say anything — you grow apart when you can't talk frequently. Tom came home in one piece after 16 months. There was quite an adjustment. The babies didn't remember him. They were scared of this strange man who wanted to play with them. Army wives and couples learn how to handle these things and understand that they are normal because everyone around them goes through similar experiences.

Tom was sent to Purdue to get his master's degree so he could teach at West Point in the Department of Military Engineering and Nuclear Science. At West Point I was again in the officers' wives' society supporting the wife of the colonel who was head of the Engineering Department. At that time wives seldom worked outside the home and Army community. There was always something going on. The West Point community was a great place, family oriented and the epitome of military life. I was confident in who I had become. I was clearly not in Kansas anymore, but I was myself and I loved it.

The Army sent us to Orléans, France. Had I not been an Army wife, I would never have had this opportunity to learn about other people, cultures, and standards of living. We lived on the economy in France, not on a military base. Learning to manage a household in a different standard of living was a challenge. From a washing machine that had to be filled and drained with a bucket, to a septic tank in our basement that overflowed because our German babysitter/housekeeper emptied her floor cleaning bucket into it and killed all the "good microbes," to learning that the lovely vegetables the landlord brought us every Sunday morning were grown in fields fertilized with human sewage — I learned and survived.

We traveled at every opportunity. The Army school where our children attended encouraged families to take children out of school to learn through travel. I loved Italy. It was musical, upbeat. Germany was clean with many entertainment opportunities for families. France seemed dreary and dark. In Orléans there were great social class distinctions between the poor and the "chateau" class.

The Army community in France was colorblind. There was an African American officer and his wife from Washington, DC, who were an integral part of our social life in France. However, when we returned to live in Washington, DC, in the 1960s, we could not socialize as we did abroad. I am grateful for the tolerance and acceptance I learned in France, not only of the Europeans, but of our own African Americans.

When I visit Kansas City now, I can see the contrast of my life experience and that of friends who continued to live in the Midwest. I have friends all over the world. Being an Army wife is a life unto itself. You get out of it what you put into it. I put in a lot and received back even more. My dad was afraid for me to marry into the Army. He feared I would lead an improper life — have to cow-tow to the General's wife. However, I found the Army to be a mutually supportive community. People were friendly because everyone was in the same boat. The Army opened up my world.

A Life Fulfilled
by
Margo Davis

"I have $60 and I'm registering for the Three-year Nursing Program in the U.S. Cadet Nurse Corps." The rather imposing woman across the counter replied, "You are going to the Scholarship Bureau and tell them I sent you."

It was January 1944. Students talked to a person when registering for college. The person across the counter was Katherine Densford, the Director of the University of Minnesota School of Nursing. Due to Miss Densford's recommendation, I needed financial assistance for only one quarter to finish prerequisites for the Five-year Nursing Program. A $150 scholarship from the Kellogg Foundation and Business and Professional Women and my $60 sufficed.

When I left high school my ambition to go on the stage met with reality — it took talent and rejection to be the next Kathryn Hepburn. For two-and-a-half years I attended two colleges, night school, worked for the Works Progress Administration (WPA), the National Youth Administration (NYA), and a bank where I advanced to 43 cents per hour.

Helping the War Effort was next. I chose the Red Cross Nurse's

Aides because they had the cutest uniforms and, I thought, delivered mail and passed trays to patients — nursing was of no interest to me.

The introductory class was on bed baths and enemas: this required me to grow up or fail. I persevered and loved nursing. At the end of the six-week training, I knew I was going back to school to be a nurse.

After Pearl Harbor and declaration of WWII in December 1941, hospitals and schools of nursing were seriously depleted of nurses and other staff. Ohio Congresswoman Frances P. Bolton introduced H.R. Bill 2326 on March 29, 1943. This bill provided for "the training of nurses for the armed services, governmental and civilian hospitals, health agencies and war industry for the duration." North Carolina Senator Josiah Bailey added the phrase which barred "discrimination in regard to race, creed or color" (H.R. Bill 2326). President Roosevelt signed the legislation on June 15, 1943. My nurses training could be funded by this bill.

The U.S. Public Health Nurse Corps was established that July. This was my opportunity. Students in that program received tuition, fees, books, hospital uniforms and housing. In addition, street dress uniforms for summer and winter were supplied, plus a $20 monthly stipend. The University of Minnesota enrolled and graduated more Cadet Nurses than any other school between 1943 and 1948 when the Corps was disbanded.

At this time when nurses were in great demand, our training included many innovations and continuing development. Because our school was also part of the University of Minnesota Medical School, student nurses participated in many procedures and treatments. These advanced opportunities helped us discover our strengths and interests.

World War II ended and our five-year class finished hospital training in September 1946. I was released from further obligation to serve the Corps and the Corps was released from paying for the remainder of my education. But, life was good. As a graduate nurse I could now work for pay and I could borrow money from the University for tuition to complete my last three quarters until graduation.

I began my nursing career in the newborn nursery and moved on to Public Health where I continued to "learn by doing." When my children were all very young, I volunteered: teaching health to Girl Scouts and homemakers, and working with bloodmobiles. My remarkably cooperative children deserve full credit for my early ability to extend my activities beyond the home. They brought up themselves and each other when I wasn't there.

We lived in New England for 25 years. There, small towns with limited resources couldn't afford to hire specialists for many projects. Instead, residents were appointed to serve on committees and boards. My work as a Public Health Nurse and my involvement with the League of Women Voters was visible to the community and the Town Moderator appointed me to my first, of many, community projects. My education and nursing experience gave me confidence in my ability and judgment to promote programs and work with people. I accepted the appointment.

This community work included being responsible for selecting professional and technical resources for building schools and a hospital, dealing with budgets and results, as well as overall supervision of programs and reporting to authorities. I found it to be a unique, stimulating and often frustrating experience. Usually, I was the only one with a medical background on those voluntary, unpaid bodies. There were times when a strong will and dedication was needed to proceed with a project. I found it satisfying to be both a Hospital Trustee and Chairman of the Hospital Building Committee. It was devastating to "fight City Hall" as Chairman of the committee dealing with drugs, delinquency and alcohol among teenagers.

After leaving New England, my husband and children all grew up and left my nest. It was a new era for women. I worked for the Equal Rights Amendment (ERA), supported Displaced Homemakers, pursued Gerontology (which was a new field at the University level), and worked in Wellness Clinics. Eventually, it was time to retire and travel. I enjoyed that immensely until three of my family were killed and another seriously injured by a drunk driver.

I took on the overpowering enterprise of becoming a Victim's Advocate to work for legislation both to prevent driving under the influence and to support the needs of the victims of alcohol related accidents through the courts. For years I concentrated on this scourge of society. Yet it continues to be another serious medical and social issue.

I hope Miss Densford (whose recommendation helped me continue my education at a critical time for me) knew, in her wisdom, how much I benefited from her help and guidance. Long after her retirement I met Miss Densford in an airport and gratefully thanked her for her contribution to my life.

Later in my life a mystery about Miss Densford was clarified for me by a follow resident at La Vida Llena, the life care community where I had moved. In 1945 I missed my last opportunity to learn from Miss Densford when she was "missing in action" from a course I was assigned to take. When I moved to La Vida Llena I learned the reason from Lt. Col. Nina "Bennie" Baker, RN. Miss Densford had been abruptly ordered to conduct an Inspection Tour to assess nurses living and working conditions throughout France and Nina Baker had been her guide. After this lengthy tour Miss Densford had given Nina a small picture of herself with a note, on the back, thanking Bennie for a good job and for her conscientious support. I sent this memento to the University of Minnesota when they were establishing a memorial to Miss Densford.

In 2009 the University of Minnesota School of Nursing celebrated the Centennial of its founding and selected 100 Distinguished Alumni. I was humbled to be included. Miss Densford's support and the knowledge and skills I learned through nursing led me there. I am proud of this award which was given to Margaret Horton-Davis who was "recognized for her years of community and volunteer service, victims' advocacy, promotion of youth development and women's rights, support of education with learning disabilities, proactive commitment to providing a healthy environment, safe schools, better sanitary conditions and well equipped hospital facilities." (University of Minnesota Nursing Alumni Society, November 5, 2009)

Camp Natarswi: A Lasting Impact on My Life
by
Hélène "Lanie" Dickel

The Maine Girl Scout Camp, Natarswi, has had a great impact on my life. My best friends were made at camp and I learned outdoor life skills and the love of nature that have lasted a lifetime.

Natarswi, though sounding like an Indian name, is actually short for **Nat**ure, **Ar**chery, and **Swi**mming! It began in 1936 and just celebrated its 75th year. Camp Natarswi is a 30-acre rustic camp located within the boundaries of Baxter State Park about 18 miles from Millinocket, Maine. It sits on Lower Togue Pond with the majestic Mt. Katahdin beyond. Mt. Katahdin is the highest mountain in Maine and is the beginning (or end) of the Appalachian Trail.

In the summers since I was born, our family spent the whole summer at our cottage on Mount Desert Island, Maine. My sister, Lin was 13 and I, Lanie, was 11 when my mother's psychiatrist recommended that we kids should go to camp (in part to give my mother a much-needed break). Thus it was that we and several other girls from Southwest Harbor were driven to Bangor and then in a camp bus to Natarswi. Lin and I were in different units. It was raining the day we arrived and my tent leaked a bit. No mountain was visible. But, in spite of that, we stayed four weeks that first year and loved it enough to return every year thereafter for the full camp season of six weeks.

When I was 14, I was in the Junior Maine Guide unit. We lived out on the *Point*, built our own latrine and wash basin stand, and then washed our clothes and ourselves in the lake (not allowed any more in our now environmentally conscientious world). We planned, prepared and cooked our own meals over the fire, except for going to the main camp dining room once a week. We learned how to handle an axe. We perfected our swimming — taking the Junior Red Cross Life Saving course, and learned to paddle a canoe — in tandem and solo. Each summer we climbed Mt. Katahdin (one mile high) and took several wilderness canoe camping trips. We bonded with each other in the unit and with our counselors whom we adored.

When I was a teenager, the elementary grades and the four-year high school were in the same building. There were 30 students in my class; I and another girl were Wheaton College Faculty brats and good friends. I was smart but shy. There was a bit of town/gown distinction (unspoken) so I had few real friends during most of the year — but…when I went to Camp Natarswi for six weeks, there were the friends from the year before and new ones to be made. Without Camp Natarswi, I would have been miserable as a teenager with no social life. As a result, the friends I made at camp became my lifeline to happiness and sanity. That is the first and perhaps the most important impact it had on my life from the beginning. A couple of camp friends also went to Mt. Holyoke College. I've kept in touch with many of them over the years and see one of them every summer as she has a Maine cottage within an hour's drive from our cottage.

The Junior Maine Guide unit also had a mission – to prepare us to go to *Testing Camp* that was held each summer for several days.

We drove in the old camp truck to some central Maine camp on a lake and for three days we were tested on our camping and water skills — making a lean-to, making a fire with one match and a wet log — the best choice was to find some *Dri Ki* on the shore. *Dri Ki* is Northern Maine for dry kindling or driftwood. The core would be dry and the log was easily split with an axe. We had to show our skill at map and compass, paddling a canoe solo in the wind, cooking including a cake in a reflector oven, etc. It was unusual to pass all the tests in the first year, but you could return the second year and complete them. It took me the two years. My sister did it in one year!

After two years in the Junior Maine Guide unit, I was ready to be a CIT – a counselor in training and then the next year I was a regular, paid counselor. I think it was my freshman year in college when I took the Red Cross Canoeing Instructors course. With this training I was able to be a Canoeing Trip Counselor at Camp Natarswi for one summer, then at private Camp Onaway in New Hampshire, and finally at the National Music Camp in Interlochen, Michigan, until my summers were spent as an astronomy graduate student at the University of Michigan. Those summers as a Canoeing/Trip Counselor were the best!

When I met John Dickel (my future husband) at the University of Michigan in the fall of 1960, one of our first dates was to go for a paddle on a nearby lake. I knew that if John didn't know how to paddle, I could handle the canoe on my own and he was thinking the same thing that he could handle the canoe. We were both pleasantly surprised and that was one of the things that cemented our relationship – along with camping and hiking as we discovered later.

When we were getting married, John's parents gave us some money for a honeymoon — with their permission we used the money to buy our first canoe together — a 16-foot wood canvas canoe which lasted many years, but not as long as our marriage! Later when we were showing John's parents how our two daughters were learning to paddle, I was sitting on the shore with his mother, Jane, and before I could mention it myself, Jane remarked, "Soon you will need two canoes [– pause –] and I'll buy you the second one." The paddling and camping skills learned from Camp Natarswi (and for John, at Camp Keewaydin in Vermont) were passed along to our two girls and now to our grandchildren. Our granddaughter Grace attended Camp Natarswi for a week when she was only 8 years old. What a lasting effect, Camp Natarswi has had on the Ramseyer and Dickel and now Upham families!

The University of Illinois students living in Snyder Hall also benefited indirectly from my experiences at Camp Natarswi. John and I were *Faculty Friends* for Snyder Hall students for many years. We had dinner with them in their residence hall once or twice a month and at our home for make-it-yourself pizza and playing games twice a year. In addition, in October we would take them on an all-day outing to a nearby State Park and rent canoes for a paddle, followed by a picnic among the fall colors. In May before the semester exams, we'd usually go on an overnight camping and paddling trip with a group of them.

I would not trade my eight years at Camp Natarswi for the world. My life has been enriched by this camping experience. My sister and I still love to return to Camp Natarswi and become *campers* again during special anniversary weekend celebrations at the end of the regular camp season. We've been back to three such weekends.

A Lucky Grandchild

by
Jean Dilley

Since I was the first grandchild, my grandfather took me under his wing and we became great pals, you might say. We lived in adjacent houses, so we often spent time together which was very fortunate for me. My grandfather was a brilliant man, an engineer listed in "Who's Who in America," and to me he seemed to know about everything. Often we would take walks in the woods near our houses, and Grampa would show me all sorts of things — the wild flowers, the trees, the occasional bugs, and tell me what their names were and how, in some cases, they were used. I got to know that Spring Beauties were the first flowers to bloom; then the Adders Tongues; and shortly after, the May Apples with their canopies of leaves that hid the small white flowers. In the low, marshy spots we'd find Skunk Cabbage. And if we were lucky we'd find a few Jack-in-the-Pulpits and some trillium. I also could identify the oaks, maples, dogwood and many more trees. The woods are long gone now, as are our houses. Though I lived in the Southwest for many years later in my life, when I returned to the eastern part of the country to live, I delighted in recognizing those eastern species.

Grampa must have found in me some characteristics that he encouraged by reading to me, and then helping me to read by myself. He enjoyed my independence, my curiosity about all sorts of things, and that I was a quick learner. He taught me how to use the dictionary and enjoyed using big words that I learned to pronounce. We'd laugh over my efforts to say "cinnamon" correctly. He even made up long words, one example of which was his greeting to me: "How does your coporosity segaciate with your diabolical system of your cofugelty?" Which simply meant "How are you?" We'd laugh over this silly greeting that I've remembered all my life. Soon my favorite gifts were books.

We were a big family and at holiday gatherings, especially at Christmas, I always got a new supply of books. Among my favorites were the "Twin Series": the "Dutch Twins," the "French Twins," the "Indian Twins," etc. That got me started on wanting to travel when I grew up and actually spend time in other countries where I could meet new people and see how they lived, worked, even prayed, as I knew that there were beliefs different from ours.

All that and the fact that Grampa and Nanny took a trip by boat around the world when I was about 5 added to my interest in traveling. When they returned the steamer trunk sat in the hall for several weeks and I was allowed to forage through some of the drawers where I found caches of things that they'd brought back from their travels. I still remember a carved olivewood donkey from Israel and a shiny oval nutmeg from somewhere in the Far East. Eventually several gorgeous Oriental rugs that they'd bought to fit the living room, hall, and dining room, arrived. I wanted to know how they were made and how they produced the lovely colors and designs. Wanting to see the world and its people came naturally from all of this.

We also had cottages on Lake Erie, where summers were spent, and there Grampa and I continued our wanderings along the shore of the lake. I learned some things about geology on those walks since Grampa would pick up a stone and explain something about its origin. Depending on how brutal the weather had been — how big the storms on the lake had been — sometimes we would find that the beach had disappeared over the winter and the underlying clay was exposed. That provided a new source to investigate because the clay was full of small holes where stones had been washed out.

We poked through these holes and found coins and nails, and once, we found a small gold ring. These heavier pieces sank to the bottom of the holes, sometimes covered with sand. There was a lesson for me in that discovery. The power of the waves also ruined cottages situated too close to the edge of the water. With each storm more of a cottage would be gone forever.

We would watch the groups of sanderlings behaving like sewing machines as they foraged for tiny bits of food, their heads bobbing up and down as they moved over the sand and retreated from the next wave. In swampy areas along the edge of the water, we could see great blue herons stalking with purpose, intent on stabbing an unwary fish.

Bird watching eventually became one of the delights of my life. There is scarcely a place on earth where there are no birds; so seeing and identifying birds all over the world was another area of curiosity that my grandfather encouraged.

I often think of Grampa since I still use a leather-bound dictionary that he gave my mother before I was even born. He had found my mother to be all that he expected her children would be, and was so proud to have her in the family when she married his son. What a start in life he provided me; one that pointed me in wonderful directions for the rest of my life. Thank you so much, Grampa, for your companionship during the few years we had together before you died when I was just seven.

The Sea of Galilee
by
Barbara Fentiman

"As Jesus walked beside the Sea of Galilee, he saw Simon and his brother Andrew casting a net into the lake, for they were fishermen. 'Come, follow me,' Jesus said, 'and I will make you fishers of men.' At once they left their nets and followed him." Mark 1:16-18

"When he saw that they were straining at the oars against an adverse wind, he came towards them early in the morning, walking on the sea. He intended to pass them by. But when they saw him walking on the sea, they thought it was a ghost and cried out; for they all saw him and were terrified. But immediately he spoke to them and said, 'Take heart, it is I; do not be afraid.'" Mark 6:48-50

Sunday, April 23, 2006, was a beautiful day in The Holy Land and I was in a fishing boat on the Sea of Galilee. Jesus had been especially active in this area and that thought never left my mind. I am where Jesus was; I am on the water on which he walked! The entire Holy Land experience was an emotional one for me, but the Sea of Galilee was the most moving, soul-stirring and unforgettable. What

made it so awe-inspiring was the close relationship Jesus had with this area. It was easy to picture him and the disciples on the water in their fishing boats. The Sea of Galilee, which is really a fresh water lake, is beautiful as is the countryside surrounding it. The Sea and the fertile valleys surrounding the Sea have been called an earthly Garden of Eden. It is completely encircled by a beach, bordered by escarpments on the east and southwest and by plains on the north and northwest. The Sea is 13 miles long and seven miles wide and lies 675 feet below sea level. It was made even more poignant for me because its bed forms a part of the Great Rift Valley which is the same rift, I was told, which I so loved during my years of living in East Africa.

One of the most intriguing finds from the time of Jesus is an ancient boat found in the Sea. The boat sank nearly two thousand years ago and is a rare example of the kind of boat in which Jesus would have sailed. Based on several criteria, the boat is firmly dated to the first centuries B.C.-A.D. We were able to view the boat, which has been restored, and I chose to believe that this was a boat from which Jesus and his disciples had fished.

It is not by chance that these scenic shores provided the backdrop for so many important events in the life of Jesus. By its waters he chose his first disciples, healed the sick and preached the gospel of the Kingdom. The Gospels record that Jesus walked on the Sea of Galilee to join his disciples in a boat and on another occasion he spoke to a storm to calm the wind and waves. His disciples wondered: *"Who then is this, that even the wind and the sea obey him?"* We had no wind that day, but the scene was vividly clear in my mind.

I knew of the Sea of Galilee and the story of Jesus walking on water all my life. However, as I sat in the prow of the boat gazing out over the water, it became clear to me what I was seeing, and the impact was profound. This was where Jesus had lived and worked teaching the people the word of God. He breathed the same air I was breathing and was on the same water I was on, albeit I was sitting on that water in a boat while he walked on it. It was a deeply spiritual moment and that moment in time has remained with me.

We had a very special worship service while crossing the Sea and sang hymns. It ended with the boat captain raising the American flag (next to the Israeli flag) and playing the Star Spangled Banner. Goosebumps for sure!

Our little boat floated onto the beach at Tiberias and I walked on the sand (again, where Jesus walked?) feeling refreshed, rejuvenated, renewed, invigorated, stimulated and strengthened. I felt I was awakened to the glories of God and when I returned home, I pursued this invigorated Barbara with the goal of being a more kind, loving, helpful and spiritual person (no more temper tantrums!). I will always have to continue working towards this goal, of course, but the experience that April day on the Sea of Galilee has prompted me not to just "read" the Bible, but to "study" it and decipher what it was that Jesus was truly saying when he was preaching and teaching to the multitudes. Those lessons learned can be humbling but most rewarding.

My story here is short, but I will carry with me always the beauty, calmness, peacefulness and, most of all, the lessons learned from the Sea of Galilee and the experience of knowing it which so enriched my life.

April 30, 1940
by
Christiane Fiquet-Bart

The German tanks are advancing at great speed towards Normandy.

During the night my parents decide that Mother and we children, ages 14, 12, 6, and 3, should leave in the morning. So the family car is loaded with suitcases and off we go for an "adventure" trip. Leaving everything behind is very traumatic. Father would not leave until the troops reached the town. We see him again in Brittany where we are staying with friends. From there we continue our "adventure" to Perigord, in the center of France.

One day we receive a letter telling us that the house has been bombed — the only one in town. There are no details, except that the bombing came 30 minutes after Father left the house. Now we are quite anxious to go back "home" as soon as possible.

The return trip is difficult. We cross devastated places, some hard to recognize. Furthermore, getting gas takes a lot of time as we find long lines of cars waiting to get to the pumps. Finally after a few days we are standing in front of the house. What a sad sight! The foundations are displaced by almost a yard and there are large cracks in the walls everywhere. Two bombs had fallen — one on each side of the house. Only my parents accompanied by firemen can enter. A friend living in a large house gives us shelter, as his family is not yet back from the south of France.

The following days are a challenge for everyone. My parents salvage as much furniture as they can, but find hardly any linen, china, books, paintings, photos, etc. We are amazed that we find the concert piano worth saving, but it will need repairs as does other furniture. In the kitchen the refrigerator is covered with bricks and debris. When the debris is removed and it is plugged in, to our great surprise, it works. After three hours, we have ice! During the occupation we have a battered, but working, refrigerator. We appreciate being able to keep food longer when we can get it. One day I see a small porcelain doll hanging from an attic beam outside. It is sad to see it helplessly perched up high. A very kind fireman climbs on his tall ladder and brings it to me. Everyone tries to help so much.

Now it is time to destroy the house because the cracks are getting wider. In the morning I see equipment nearby, but all I remember is the house crashing down on the ground in a huge cloud of dust. All that is left are piles of bricks and debris. I will never forget it. Mother is very depressed, more than before. She is so attached to everything we had. It is gloom all the time. And now we have to look for a new abode. We locate a fairly large house that would fit all of us. It is surrounded by lawns and tall trees. But, unfortunately it is occupied by the army. The mayor pleads to the Kommantur to release it; so finally after several days of discussion, the house is vacant. The next problem is to secure materials to renovate the whole house. Commerce is at a standstill and we have to do with what is in stock in town. Mother does a good job as a decorator and this new project keeps her somewhat away from her depression.

After a while we resume a fairly normal life in this new home and I start to reflect on the last months since April 30, 1940, when we left Normandy. I do not want to become attached to material things in my life because nothing is forever. Like for everything on the planet, material things come and go. My family is safe and well. That is the most important thing for which we can be very happy. Since my teenage years I have never deviated from this way of thinking.

A Surprise Arrival
by
June Fischer

Probably the event which changed the course of my life the most was the birth of my fourth child, a beautiful baby of nine and one half pounds. The big surprise was that he was born with Down syndrome. Kenneth Robert Fischer had arrived. At first I thought how fortunate I was to have three bright "normal" children. In my first years of marriage I thought it would be so nice to have a family of two boys  and two girls. Two boys and one little girl were already here as part of the plan. And now they had a baby brother!

The first six weeks were a struggle for his life. Instead of gaining weight he steadily lost his excess pounds until he was down to six pounds. We were told by the doctor that he probably could not survive. But he did. After his baptism he recovered and was on his way to becoming the lovely 50-year-old person he is today.

At first I had to spend many hours each day holding a bottle. Because of the formation of his mouth he was very slow and could not be nursed. He was a 1-year-old before he could sit up alone and 3 before he could walk. His first word was "Mama" at 5. At 13 he learned how to read and would bring books home from the library. One of his books was Tolstoy's "War and Peace." He could sound out the words when I asked him what they were. As a family we did a lot of camping in various states and places from Maine to Virginia. He was very adventurous and made friends for all of us on these family trips. As time went on into his teens, he became an excellent swimmer and participated in Special Olympics. He was selected to go to Madison Square Garden in New York City where he participated in a dancing marathon. He loved to dance with all of his teachers and friends and fancied himself as another Fred Astaire. However, he was so enthralled with New York City he wanted to return. He filled a jar with coins, took my car keys off the hook and did not get any further than the garage door, which he could not open — nor could he drive a car. He was 17 at the time. Over the years there were many adventures, each one challenging. He enjoyed moving furniture. One day when I walked into the living room after shopping, all the furniture was in a different place, except for my grand piano.

For many years after he was an adult, Kennie was able to travel on the airlines. It was most often to places that I had traveled to: where the other children were then living, or where we were vacationing. We would go to the airport and there he would be waiting for us -- ready to have a happy time. He never seemed upset when it was time to go back home because he loved to fly and was happy to be wherever he was. When asked if he liked one place or one person more than another he would say he liked everybody the same. If you wanted a yes or no answer, he would say, "Maybe yes."

Kennie loved music and I was not concerned when one day I heard him playing the piano in the living room. It was a small grand with ivory keys. To my dismay when I looked to see what was happening, he had taken the poker from the fireplace and was busily hitting the keys with it. They were all broken, but I had them repaired with plastic keys. My oldest son repaired the woodwork to look like new, and I traded it in for a new Baldwin grand.

Kennie's learning abilities were always over a longer learning period than a normal child's. But he did learn. With many years of speech therapy, which he seemed to enjoy, he learned how to speak more clearly. Babyhood lasted longer, being a toddler lasted longer, and being an adolescent lasted longer. He wanted to do what others could do and was often thwarted in the attempt.

Kennie was very good at disappearing from my sight when I was with him. When he was about 5, I took him to a mall with me to shop for a new Easter hat. I tried on one hat after another until I looked down at the stroller and Kennie was not in it. Nor was he anywhere in the store that I was quickly searching. I decided to go to the lost and found department only to see Kennie running up and down the aisle of the lost and found department without anyone noticing.

On another relatively quiet summer day when Kennie was not to be found in the house or neighborhood, my husband and I jumped in the car to look for him — first in the amusement park. Then I remembered he had been talking about wanting to go to California. This time he knew he could not go by car. I suggested we drive down the road in the direction of the airport which was a good 20 miles away. When we saw him walking down the road about two miles out of town, we stopped the car and called out to him. He looked around and held out his arms crying, "Mama."

When Kennie was 21 he went to live in a group home in a nearby town. My husband and I were visiting another of our children when the phone rang and we were told that Kennie had spent the night in the town jail. We were shocked and drove home to investigate. It was just before Christmas and Kennie was going to go Christmas shopping. While on the bus, which took him home from work, he had a fight with another resident. Therefore, he was told he could not go Christmas shopping. He rebelled. The staff sent for the police. The Chief of Police arrived. Kennie kicked him and the Chief put him in jail for the night. I was so upset I could have kicked the Chief of Police myself.

Kennie's health was and still is threatening his survival. His strong will to live brought him through pneumonia which had turned him blue, and through two hospitalizations with thrombosis. I knew he was getting better when the furniture was rearranged in his hospital room — bed, dresser and TV — all moved physically by a recovered Kennie.

Kennie has a strong sense of humor and often had us all laughing. I believe that growing up with Kennie brought our family many rewards. He helped in the development of our patience and perseverance, and our tolerance and understanding of people who are different from ourselves. Kennie went to school until he was 21. Then he started working at Key Industries which provided work projects for handicapped people of different levels of ability. He worked for several hours a day until he retired last year. Now he is in a daily activity program which he enjoys. He lives in a group home in the state of New York. He has traveled widely in several states, Canada, Hawaii and England, to visit wherever his family is living. However, he is unable to travel anymore because of his health. Now we use the telephone and mailman for our contacts. Kennie is not long out of my thoughts. Once a month Kennie has the florist deliver a beautiful flower arrangement to me.

Being the mother of a Down syndrome child for 50 years is certainly a large factor in the person I am today. I managed to squeeze in the time to raise my other three children, further my education, teach music to hundreds of children for 20 years in New York state schools, have traveling experiences in various countries, live in England for 14 years, and now spend my last years in the Land of Enchantment. Lucky me!

And so I can say that the event which has had the most influence on the direction of my life was the birth of my son, Kenneth Robert Fischer.

I Almost Walked on Lily Pads
by
Mary Lou Goodwin

My earliest recollection occurred when I was 3 or 4 years of age. My mother, father and I attended a group event at a lake in southern Arkansas. Water lilies completely covered the surface of the lake.

I remember my astonishment at first seeing the lake and, secondly, believing I could walk across the lily pads. Of course, when I tried some-one pulled me from the water. I don't recall going under water or being reprimanded. However, I'm sure both occurred. Still convinced that walking on lily pads should be possible, I have continued to try different experiences throughout my life.

I have loved music from my earliest days. My mother played the piano. We attended church as a family where I loved the hymns and the caring support of the congregation. Music lessons, from Mrs. Kilpatrick in Tyler, Texas, in fourth grade introduced me to classical music. Public school music appreciation classes in fifth and sixth grades introduced me to American and folk music. I still love the Welsh lullaby, "All Through the Night," "William Tell Overture," the songs of Stephen Foster, and many other pieces of music. Being the mother of four children and the wife of a minister, music became my solace and stress reliever. I played my repertoire most nights after putting the children to bed.

I met the love of my life, BC, in a race relations class in 1947 as a junior student at Southern Methodist University in Dallas. We married in 1949, while he was enrolled at Perkins School of Theology. Some members of my family, mainly my mother, a PK (pastor's kid) herself, cautioned against marrying a Methodist minister. I, however, having almost walked on lily pads, saw it as a great opportunity and challenge. I embraced my partnership in our joint ministry.

There was an occasion when the vision of lily pads strengthened our courage, but it took a tarantula to make us leap. It was the 1950s. Reverend Finis Crutchfield, BC's mentor and our good friend, had been vacationing with his family in the Colorado Rockies years before. In 1956 he discovered a property with five small, abandoned, rustic log cabins built by C.C. Smith of Kentucky. They were various sizes with two and three sleeping rooms, electricity, water and outhouses. The property had been on the market for about five years and the price had come down considerably. Finis had been trying to convince several friends to go together and buy the property. We kept saying, "No." It was not a good time for us: child #3 had just been born; we had a newly financed used car; and the cabin was 800 miles from our home.

However, we loved the outdoors and in the summer of 1957 we rented a cabin in Bartlesville, Oklahoma, just 40 miles from home. It was a nice cabin, air conditioned with indoor plumbing. As we arrived we were taken aback by a horde of tarantulas crossing the road; then the proprietors told us to be careful because they'd seen copperheads near the creek. The first night our baby was "eaten up" by mosquitoes. The weather was hot and shying away from the "obstacles" outside, we spent most of our time indoors. Finis called us again while we were vacationing to see if we would consider changing our minds about the Colorado property. We still just could not muster the courage to walk onto that particular lily pad scene. However, on our last night in the rented cabin BC climbed up the ladder to his bunk, threw back the covers and there was a tarantula ready to share his sleeping space. That was the last straw. We packed up the kids and our belongings and headed home. The next day BC called Finis and said, "Yes. I'll go look." It was one of the best decisions of our life.

We named the cabin Riverview. It has been our geographical roots as we moved to various parsonages. Its location adjacent to Rocky Mountain National Park has allowed us many hiking and camping experiences. The other families who purchased the cabins on the property became our extended family. We loved sharing stories around the campfires and laughing through many intergenerational game nights. Riverview has been our "heaven-on-earth."

BC and I moved to La Vida Llena (LVL), a retirement community in Albuquerque, New Mexico, in 2003. This was a move we knew was important for us and our children. When I was widowed in 2009, the residents and staff of LVL continued to walk with me through valleys of grief and mountains of joy. My children and grandchildren offer love and support from near and far.

I am grateful that water lilies led me to a life filled with blessings and that music continues to accompany me in times of stress. I play my favorite CDs on my Bose CD player day and night at LVL and on older equipment at our beloved Riverview in Colorado.

As the years go by and my days dwindle to a precious few, I can see BC reaching out to me as he walks on water lilies. With Beethoven's "Moonlight Sonata" and Chopin's "Nocturne in E-flat Major" playing in the background, he and I walk over lily pads to greet our friends and family waiting there. I'm sure BC will introduce me to wonderful new friends and tell new stories.

I Don't Know How to Quit
by
Colleen Hill

After searching my life for the answer to why I don't quit, I have decided that it began in very early childhood. I was born in the first Great Depression, in 1928. Since my father, who was a dentist, was employed, my mother's family all decided to live together so living expenses could be shared. Actually, first it was one part of the family, my aunt and uncle, who moved in; and then, later, my grandparents and another uncle. Finally the house with four bedrooms, but only one bathroom, held eight of us plus an uncle who used the garage as his room.

I don't remember any arguing or fighting. Everyone worked toward the goal of taking care of the family. After careful shopping and planning, the women did the cooking. My uncles worked hard to find jobs, but there were none. I remember my mother telling me later that once she saw a potato in the gutter and, although it was very dirty, she picked it up and took it home. After thorough cleaning, she cooked it. She never told anyone where it had been. She was embarrassed to even tell me about such a secret. The struggles to manage must have been many, but my family handled them without strife and always moved forward. I did not learn how to complain about hardship.

As I became more aware, as children do, I only remember the fun times. There was always someone to read to me or push me on my swing outside. We lived in Lenox, in the Los Angeles area. We always sat down for dinner together.

One evening when the table was set and the ice cubes in the water glasses, we were waiting for my father to return. All of a sudden the earth began to shake and the building swayed. It was an earthquake. Instead of staying in the house, two adults took me by the hand and we charged for the outside. My feet did not touch the ground. When we got outside we watched the telephone pole and wires sway back and forth. Fortunately, we were all safe. During those days there was no immediate news. The adults did not know how to handle the situation. There was much confusion. This was the earthquake of 1932 in Los Angeles. To watch the adults in my family pick themselves up and figure out the next move after the destruction of the earthquake was one of the first experiences I remember where I learned to pick up and move on.

I was always tall for my age and that made me different. Even then, I made a joke out of it. In high school when the kid with the locker below mine teased me — "Your arms are all over me. I'm going to call you spider." — I thought it was funny. I don't let things bother me.

The real test for me came in 1968 at County General Hospital in the large amphitheater of the University of Southern California Medical School. The doctors were explaining my medical condition to a new class of medical students. They determined I had Amyotrophic Lateral Sclerosis (ALS), often referred to as "Lou Gehrig's" disease. They told me that I had three to five years to live and that I should go home and rest. However, at the time I was working in my husband's office and I thought it was a dumb idea to just go home and rest.

I worked as long as I could file things. Computers came in and made it a little easier for me to keep going. Even in an Amigo, a mobility scooter, I worked in the office. When I finally had to stay home I could not manage alone. I needed a caretaker at home and knew I had to find someone. My children were not of an age to be able to help and I did not want them tied to home. They were in school and getting married. There were not good home health agencies like we have now. We made do with what we could find, but it became more and more difficult.

My husband finally said, "We've got to get to someplace where people can take care of you." I got busy and wrote on the computer to all kinds of places, including the Chamber of Commerce in Albuquerque, New Mexico, asking about care facilities. La Vida Llena (LVL), a life care retirement community in Albuquerque, answered the quickest and was the friendliest. They sent information. By this time, the late '80s, my husband was ready to retire. We sold the house and moved to LVL in 1993.

My husband hadn't thought we'd ever get resettled. When we came into LVL, I could only move my hands a little. I couldn't move my body below my waist. No one thought I had a lot of time. My husband had an apartment in Independent Living and I took up residence in Health Care. I could visit the apartment and any area at LVL. It was the answer for us. My husband died in 1999 from not taking good care of himself and I'm still here.

At LVL I've had good nursing aides. They are kind to me. They know what they are doing in taking care of me. Everyone is so good to me — and I am good and thankful to them. My caretakers are young enough to be my grandchildren. I was supposed to lose my voice before my hands, but that has not happened. As new diagnostic equipment, like the MRI, came into use, my doctors tried to find a new diagnosis for me. But they haven't found anything else that fits me. They continue to say I have ALS, but a very unique type.

Because I still have my mind and can think, I'm on every Health

Care committee to help keep things working well for us residents. Since being here I've never shut up. Early on, Health Care was very separate from the rest of the resident community. Then, some years ago, Health Care became part of the Resident Council and we — I — had a voice in that forum where residents manage affairs in the facility that pertain to the wellbeing of all of us. I remain involved in how things go in Health Care and at LVL. I like being on the committees that decide things important to residents. I say what matters.

Long ago, when I was still in Los Angeles, a Palm Reader said my palm had many extra wrinkles — meaning I was going to live to be really old, into my 70s and 80s. I guess I believed him. I don't know why I can't quit. I just can't.

I was diagnosed 25 years before I moved to LVL. I have been here 18 years. I'm 83 years old. I think my medical doctors have been disappointed they haven't been able to do an autopsy to discover what has really happened in my body. I tend to treat my situation as a crooked twist of fate.

My children weren't small when I was diagnosed. I had time to raise them. As a grandma I could give my grandchildren rides on my wheelchair. My granddaughter is a nurse in Sacramento, California. She is the mother of my great-grandchild. That great-granddaughter has worn the dress I wore as a child when I was a flower girl. I've had good times and good memories in my life.

Do I get discouraged? I don't think so. I can't figure that out. Perhaps it is a special gene. My whole family, my dad, had the same gene. We did not know strife and complaining. My mother adored my father. Love has always been around me. How could I possibly quit!

A Liberating Life in New Mexico
by
Carol Hjellming

In June 1976 all seven Hjellm-
ings, the family dog, and many plants
moved to Socorro, New Mexico, after
eight years living in Charlottesville,
Virginia. Bob, my husband, was an
astrophysicist with National Radio
Astronomy Observatory and wanted
to do research using the Very Large
Array telescopes on the Plains of San
Agustin, 52 miles west of Socorro.

Junior Hjellmings, three boys and
two girls, 8 to 16 years old, enrolled in four of the five city schools.
I was still a housewife and former English major. During that first
year in Socorro I started questioning what I wanted to be doing in
the next three to five years. Still making brownies and cupcakes for
schoolroom parties? Not really! In the years since "stopping out" of
college, I had turned hobbies into mini-research projects: sewing,
dying fabric, gardening, etc. No one had walked down the road to
tell me what went on in my dye pot, and only an organic gardening
book written by a chemist told why pH numbers don't go higher
than 14.

Now, in Socorro, we lived only blocks away from New Mexico
Institute of Mining and Technology (NMT). With this learning op-

portunity available in my own back yard, could I continue moaning about never having taken chemistry and not knowing anything about the chemistry of dying fabric or of gardening or of anything? Not really!

So, I went to the NMT Chemistry Department and talked to the Chem 121 teacher about whether he thought I could handle the class. He laughingly assured me he'd never lost a student in the class. However, he was not laughing when I could not remember the entire quadratic equation. That took me to the Registrar's Office where I enrolled in entry level chemistry and math (algebra) as a special, non-degree, part-time student. It was a big change after 17 years of being a housewife!

That first semester it took five days before I was thoroughly lost in the chemistry class. I closed the door on my husband's home office and literally cried — I had never before been able to read the words with no idea of the meaning! However, my courage was sustained when I received the highest score on the first math test. By the end of the semester I'd worked up to a B grade in chemistry class and A's in the chemistry lab and math class. Continuing into second semester it took five WEEKS before I was thoroughly lost again. I took that as a trend — I could do better if I persevered (I'd never worked harder in my life). I declared a Chemistry major, thereby losing my special non-degree student status. After transferring my old English major credits, NMT classified me as a senior, which allowed me the advantage of enrolling early in my freshman chemistry and physics lab sessions!

With 100 hours of transfer credits, I needed only 14 credit hours of 300-level classes to earn a Bachelor of General Studies degree. I was within striking distance of a college degree! In previous ventures into higher education I would start a course of study, but we would move before even an associate degree would be possible. This time I would do it!

It took five years. I added technical writing, ordinary differential equations, and two semesters of physical chemistry to the transferred credits. At the age of 44 and having earned a Bachelor of General Studies degree along the way, I received the desired Bachelor of Science in Chemistry *magna cum laude*. Not bad for a former English major housewife. I had five kids still at home when I became a "retread" (an older returning student) and three of them were still at home when I finished the second degree. I was the first in my immediate Johnson family to earn a college degree.

Job hunting in Socorro involved networking in the grocery stores and parking lots in addition to checking the job board in NMT Human Resources. A geologist friend called to say there was an opening in the New Mexico Bureau of Mines and Mineral Resources (NMBMMR). The position would be small to start, but had possibilities for advancement. In the interview with the Publishing Group, I admitted almost immediately that I had no secretarial skills. They breathed a sigh of relief because they didn't want an editorial secretary -- that was just the way they had to list the opening. I was hired to learn to code manuscripts for computer typesetting programs at the UNM Printing Plant.

Within a short time, working in the Publishing Group of the NMBMMR used everything I had ever learned: all the writing and grammar; all the chemistry, geochemistry and geophysics; all the math; even all the popular geology I'd learned on vacations in national parks. To that was added learning the details of production printing and bringing our office into digital production. The first atlas I edited involved more than 1,000 figures. The second atlas involved 54 geologists in five states and was supported by a grant of $1.5 million dollars. It won second place for Publication of the Year from the Awards Committee of our international professional group.

We editors were able to join and attend the annual professional meetings of the Association of Earth Science Editors (AESE). I chaired sessions, gave presentations, and served as an officer before retiring in 1999.

Completing my education enabled me to have a work identity and increased my personal confidence. It opened the opportunity for a professional job with immense professional acknowledgement from my peers. The interaction with colleagues, both professionally and socially, was rewarding and a far cry from being a mother and housewife. Earning a regular salary, even though it was not far above minimum wage at first, enabled me to think up from $0 economically. I had money of my own for the first time.

But the stress and tension of deadlines and being the middle person between writers and final publication was tough. I took the earliest exit possible while most of my body parts still worked. My husband died 15 months later, suddenly and unexpectedly. But I wasn't finished being productive. I still had goals for my retirement. During my student experience at NMT I had learned a lot about the stress of learning and living for international students, and I thought I could help them to integrate better into our English-speaking environment. I volunteered to tutor English as a Second Language. I developed the class and taught Citizenship (preparation for the naturalization interview). And I indulged my love of color by learning to quilt. I also conquered a life-long fear: I finally learned to swim at age 60 and went on to earn SCUBA Open Water Certification at 63!

Looking back on 35 years in New Mexico, I wonder if I could have done as much or accomplished as much if we had lived elsewhere — where the sun didn't shine so many days, where the sky wasn't so blue and big, where the horizons weren't so defined, where the weather wasn't so dramatic, where the sunrises and sunsets weren't so colorful. And I certainly needed and am thankful for the support of my family over these years!

As Luck Would Have It
by
Ollie Mae Hopper

I always said I was just lucky. I've always done what I wanted to do — maybe my own choices of action determined my luck. I've wondered about what would have happened in my life if I hadn't run off to get married.

I was 20 years old, about to graduate from the University of Tennessee. And I was engaged to a nice man, ten years my senior. His name was Charles and he and his brother owned a drug store. My mother was very fond of him and thought he was the ideal catch for me.

However, one night a young man, named Robert, came to a dance at our college and we danced almost every dance. He was a nice man too, *very* nice. Only four years older, he'd graduated and was working for the Tennessee Valley Authority as a civil engineer. He was also engaged — to a doctor's daughter. I liked him — a lot — and three months later, we decided to elope! We didn't *have* to get married — we just *wanted* to get married. (We were married six years before we had children.)

Well, it was a surprise to everybody. It shocked Charles. He called Mama and told her, "She'll be sorry — sorry for the rest of her life." The college paper ran a headline: "*Ollie Mae Hikes It Off to Georgia to Get Married.*"

Three male professors had me come to one of their offices and one said to me, "Ollie Mae, you don't know squat about marriage." They gave me some books on how to succeed in marital affairs. Mama gave me some advice too on how to get along with a man. She said, "When he comes home at night, don't begin telling him what went wrong that day. Just greet him and feed him, *then* you can tell him."

What's interesting, neither man was interested in my art, yet according to Mama, I was "born with a crayon in my hand." In college, I majored in Art, History and Social Studies. Political Science was my minor. But, art was my main interest and I painted and drew all the time. I graduated from the University, married or not.

When World War II came along, Bob tried to enlist, but an old high school injury kept him out. This made him feel real bad, but he volunteered to go to Pearl Harbor for some engineering work. We went to San Francisco and I stayed with him until he shipped off to Hawaii. After the war, we moved around the United States from one job to another until we moved to New Mexico and Bob had a job at Sandia Lab. Through those years, I had three children, but I still drew and painted. I kept my dream of being an artist alive. I just did it.

Bob was gone a lot on business trips and while he was gone, I'd paint. I just wanted to paint. I guess I never had sense enough to stop. When Bob came home, he'd ask, "Well, how many paintings did you do?" I'd line up all the paintings I'd done in his absence. What he liked most about them was that, by now, I was showing my work in galleries and earning money. I think that secretly he was kinda proud of me.

One time, I had a painting I'd priced at $1,500 and we delivered it to the woman who'd said she wanted it. Bob said, "Nobody is going to spend that kind of money on a painting." The woman wrote the check without batting an eye. Bob said, "Hell! Paint some more."

Another time, I was doing portraits of some local women and they'd come to the house all dressed up in evening dresses. They were sitting and posing on stools in the kitchen while I painted them. After they left, Bob said, "Get those damned women out of my kitchen – if you're going to paint, do landscapes."

So, I still had my painting career *and* my chosen husband. I was lucky. We had a good marriage. We traveled and we had a lot in common. I was *never* sorry I ran away and married him.

But the worst time in my life was 1970 when I was diagnosed with a serious heart problem. At that time no hospital in Albuquerque had the angiographic equipment for testing the heart and the doctors held out little hope. I was hospitalized and according to their monitors they thought I had three months to live. But Presbyterian Hospital knew about a hospital in Texas that had cardiac testing equipment. Taken by ambulance and carrying oxygen, I was loaded onto a plane headed to Houston. My doctor there was Dr. Denton Cooley, a well-known heart specialist. After all the tests he said I needed to keep nitroglycerin with me at all times. Taking it would keep me alive. Now I wear a patch that feeds it to me all day.

I did what Dr. Cooley told me and here I am 41 years later, a widow, but still painting and by golly – I just sold another one, "Bright Flowers." Don't you think I'm lucky?

Memoirs of a Childhood
in France During the Occupation
by
Jeannine Hudson-Green

I was 7 years old when World War II started for me. In France, August 25th is "name day" for people named Louis or Louise (named after Saint Louis). As my mother's name was Louise, this should have been a happy day celebrated with flowers, dinner at a restaurant, maybe the theater afterwards. But on August 25, 1939, we did not celebrate. My father, who was a sergeant in the Reserves, received or-  ders that day to report for duty in the French army. So my first recollection of the war is my mother crying, her head down on folded arms, holding onto the railing of the stairs outside our apartment door as my father disappears into the dark spiral of the circular staircase. France declared war on Germany September 3, 1939.

My father arranged for my mother and me to stay in the southeast of France so we would not be in Paris in case the Germans invaded it. As a soldier, my father was an "aerostier" (a balloonist) of a hot air balloon used to observe the enemy lines. A soldier was an easy target up in his gondola; so, of course, my mother worried. As young children do, I felt her worry, so I worried too. We lived for his letters, desperate to know that he was well. He sent us a tiny photo of himself. We thought he was so handsome in his uniform! The photo was on our nightstand in the bedroom that we shared with a cousin and her two children.

In June the next year, France capitulated to Germany. Everyone was heartbroken to admit defeat. The Germans were allowed to occupy what they wanted of France. At first they only wanted the northeastern areas, including Paris, so we could have stayed where we were. My father was discharged from the army and went back to Paris. So here we were: my father north of the Demarcation Line and we were south of it. People were allowed to come into occupied territory, but not out of it. If we went to be with my father we would lose the freedom that we had in the southern countryside. My mother did not hesitate. She chose to return to her husband. Many other people made similar decisions. We took the train to Paris.

Now there were German soldiers with guns in the streets with us. They had all the power and we had no rights. They could arrest you if they did not like the look on your face. My mother told me that when I was in the presence of any German, I should avoid eye contact and if possible not say anything. Be polite and quiet. My life or the lives of others around me might depend on it.

People still needed to live and so we found our way back to daily life. People resumed their jobs. We were able to get back into our old apartment. All we had to do now was get used to the look and feel of this Paris: lots of German soldiers in the streets, almost no cars except the ones used by the Germans, blackened and taped windows, the threat of bombings, the ugly red flags with the big black swastika flying over the main buildings, very limited gas and electricity, food rationing, and standing in food lines.

Everything was rationed: not just gas and electricity; but coal, heating oil, clothing, shoes and mostly food. You were given stamps which allowed you to buy some meat, some milk, some bread – but not much. Fresh vegetables and fruit were hard to come by. Because I was a child I was allowed two cups of milk per week; so I had to walk with my small pitcher, stand in line at the "laiterie" (milk shop) and walk back trying not to spill a drop. We had no way of buying ahead since we were limited to only what little amounts were allowed by our food stamps.

We tried not to go out on the streets unless we had to and were not allowed to be out after curfew. You could get searched anytime and you could not complain. But it was not just the Germans we were afraid of. There were many French who were collaborators. You never trusted anyone you did not know extremely well. Your neighbor might tell on you if he heard you say something negative about the Germans or if he heard you listening to the BBC. My schoolmates did not invite me to their apartments after school and I did not invite them to ours. One hurried home right after school.

There were still pleasant things to see and do in Paris. I remember the merry-go-round and its music that would come once or twice a year. Also there was a small circus that would perform occasionally. In the park there were Sunday concerts of light classical music — cheerful and uplifting. We tried to ignore the German soldiers who liked to participate as well.

German soldiers were everywhere. Some were on leave, but those who were on duty marched in step. Their "goose-stepping"– lifting their legs straight out in front with their heavy boots – made an unpleasant sound. One could hear them marching many blocks away. I remember one night when my father, mother and I had missed the last Métro after visiting with friends. We had to walk home through deserted, dark, silent streets. We hurried, holding hands, not saying a word. My father guided us along the small streets. We were almost home when we heard it: the dreaded goose-step. I can still hear it today in my mind. My father guided us away from the patrol and we made it safely home.

You can guess that my father was like a hero to me. My mother was my best friend. The three of us were very close. Perhaps it was in part because the outside world was threatening and frightening. We were of a loving nature, the three of us, and we were able to hug and kiss and laugh together. We were happy together in spite of the war, in spite of the cold and the lack of fancy food.

There was always music in our house to brighten us up. My mother loved to sing and taught me to enjoy singing. She would hear a tune on the radio and memorize it. She passed on her love of music to me.

Finally, it was 1944 and German troops were retreating in Russia and in North Africa. Our hopes were high. Shortly after my 12th birthday, on June 6, 1944, American and British troops landed in Normandy. Free French troops joined them and little by little pushed the Germans away. You can't imagine how happy we were. Not just happy, we were ecstatic! Yet, we were afraid at the same time. German troops were under orders to hold Paris at all costs. My father could not stand idle and not help with the fighting, so he joined the Free French Fighters. He would contact us as often as he could. We were lucky he returned to us unhurt. The fighting in Paris did not last more than a few days. Paris was liberated in August 1944.

Our only serious problem then was lack of food. This was the one and only time when we were really out of food. Because of the battle in the streets of Paris, all the stores were closed. Food could not reach Paris as the roads were used for military purposes. My father came to the rescue again. He had heard that a vegetable truck had managed to get into Paris and he knew where. I was allowed to go with him. After a long walk we found the truck — full of cabbages. We were allowed one cabbage per person. We ate cabbage for several days.

The war ended in May 1945, just before my 13th birthday. I could have come out of this time a bitter, angry young lady with hatred in my heart — but I didn't. I did learn some important lessons, which remained with me through my life and have helped to shape my character. From an early age, I learned to be responsible and to work hard. I learned to be helpful and compassionate. I emerged from this awful time with hope, confidence and enthusiasm because of my parents' care and attention. I learned to appreciate the good times, not to take them for granted. I was very lucky in many ways: no one in my family was killed or taken away and, as a consequence of the war, my family met and made friends with a young American named Craig Hudson, who would later become my husband.

Adapted with permission from *The Jeannine Françoise Dumas Hudson Story* ©*July 2010*

She Was Not a Witch
by
Mari-Luci Jaramillo

Various people and particular incidents influenced me in many ways when I was growing up. Like most young people, I was aware of very little outside of what I was interested in. I am sure that many events and many people were impacting my life, as well as, helping me change how I viewed myself, my family, the world, and my role in life. All those changes made me who I am today. However, it is extremely difficult to assign a specific value to any one incident or any one person in particular. But I am going to try to do just that.

I was 11 years old and my family was as poor as they come. How I wanted to be able to contribute something to help us, but I was too young and had no apparent skills to earn money. During this desolate time, my family moved near a small bakery. There I met one of the first persons outside my family that I came to love, admire and respect. The lady was named Clara Baasch. She was old and extremely handicapped — using both a cane and a crutch to move her large body. The neighborhood kids were mean and called her a witch. They mockingly ran away from her as though scared to death of her when they saw her. I immediately felt sorry for her and befriended her the best I could. We quickly became friends and one day she hired me to clean her little bakery and store. I could not believe my good fortune. I was going to work for this totally handicapped person with a fierce determination to be her own woman and earn her own living. I was going to learn lots from this woman, although I did not know it at the time. What a model of strength and independence she was to me. What a lucky child I was to have been in her path.

I was her errand girl and did whatever needed to be done. In addition to working every Saturday during the school year, I worked during the summer. I scrubbed the painted ceilings and walls throughout her house with scalding hot water and plenty of soap. She taught me how to clean although my hands would get red and there was no lotion to help the horrible burning feeling I endured. I scrubbed the porches in her house, including the one in the front of the store which covered the sidewalk. Sometimes, if there was time and she did not need other kinds of help, I even had to scrub her coal bin in the basement. I got paid the grand sum total of 50 cents a day. But what I learned from this friend was invaluable. Not only was she handicapped and had to endure all the suffering that goes with the condition, but she told me about the rivalry between her and her petite beautiful sister. Ms. Baasch was a big, dark skinned, not very handsome woman and she was often told so to her face. Her sister was admired for her beauty. This created an unhealthy division between the two sisters. But nothing deterred Ms. Baasch. She had a strong work ethic. During her lifetime working in that small bakery and store in our poor community, she managed to save enough money to visit Rome. What fortitude and guts that woman had. What a role model she was for me, even though I did not know it at the time. I had not even heard about role models.

For me, she was a master teacher. I learned from her many work skills, about personal responsibility, and so much about economics, i.e. "You have to save at least 25 cents from every dollar you ever earn." Of course I could not do that at the time, but I know it stayed in my mind. At the time, I turned in the weekly 50 cents I earned working on Saturday to help support our struggling family. When I grew up I probably saved money because of her example. At that young age, I also learned many social skills and social graces that she taught me by example. I even learned how to make tea and serve it elegantly to her bridge partners. These social skills became my special forte when I grew up and my friends often said I was very diplomatic in my dealings with people. I had an advantage — I had learned diplomacy when I was a little girl.

Eighth grade graduation was a big deal in my community — few of the students made it to that point and the majority who did, dropped out at that level. Because it was an important occasion, all the girls talked about getting new dresses and shoes. I knew I would not get a store-bought anything, so I was not into those plans.

When Ms. Baasch asked me what I was going to wear, I told her that I was not going to wear anything new. I would wear one of my homemade skirts and blouses. She then told me she had a beautiful dress made of silk that she had brought from Rome and did not wear anymore. She said maybe my mom could make me a dress from that material. I could not believe my ears. She gave me the dress made of cream-colored silk with tiny pink and yellow flowers and pale green leaves and vines. I loved it and ran home to tell Mom. Mom took the dress apart, washed and pressed the silk, and made me a lovely dress with a Peter Pan collar and a wide sash with a big bow on the back (so I would not look so skinny). I never felt so elegant in my life. I was a hit and many of my friends admired my dress. Ms. Baasch had a way of knowing exactly what and when to do things for others.

That singular experience, during my childhood and early teen years, of working with this incredible woman placed me in a very different path from the one I was on. My path would have been aspiring for not much more than finding a way to survive day by day. I could have found a job when older at the Five and Dime store. Because of her, I acquired new skills and many of my newfound dreams about what I wanted to be when I grew up. I learned to look at the world and myself differently. I was able to internalize the difference between my home and the rest of the world. Because of her teachings, I decided that I wanted to actively and genuinely be part of both. She had sent me on my way.

A Wake for Eric
by
Kay Johnson

Our son, Eric, died of a heart attack at the age of 44. He was never married and had no children. Eric was sitting in a dentist's chair in Arvada, Colorado, when it happened.

The dentist visit was his final task before leaving the next day to drive to Louisiana to spend Christmas 2002 with us. His long-time friend, Lisa, had driven him to the appointment, because he wasn't supposed to drive himself home. She waited for some time, then an ambulance arrived, paramedics rushed in, Eric went out on a gurney. The staff hesitated to tell Lisa anything because she wasn't a relative. She finally found out which hospital he was headed for, and she followed. In the end, it was Eric's even longer-time friend, Dave, who had the horrible job of phoning us — Eric's parents, Kay and Ralph — to tell us Eric had died. What a job for a young man to have to do! Dave didn't know a great deal, only that Eric had been without oxygen for some 23 minutes. Nobody lives after that length of time. Eric was placed on a respirator and life support equipment, because he'd long since filled out the appropriate paperwork for organ donation.

We flew to Denver, rented a huge old van because that was what was available, and drove to the Arvada hospital. We were met by Lisa and her husband, Howard. We saw Eric, very still in his very white bed in a very white room. The sun was streaming through the window making the stark white walls and sparkling floor whiter than seemed possible, and turning Eric's motionless face a warm tan. His hair looked freshly washed and was fanned out around his head. His chest was moving up and down, air was moving into him and back out of him, but his stillness said he was no longer there. Death of a child is a horror to any parent, but since then I have learned that, by far, death is not the worst thing that can happen to a deeply loved and respected offspring.

The next morning we went to the hospital to visit our young man child who was so terribly absent. Machinery running, graphs charting, chest rising and falling, and he most certainly was not present. One of the best, of the many awful, things going on happened while we were there. A youngish woman came in and introduced herself as a hospital doctor who was assigned to turn off all the machinery and check to see if there were any signs of life remaining. Brain waves had not been recorded since Eric entered the hospital. She offered us the option of leaving the room, but we chose to stay. She spoke to Eric in the most personal, thoughtfully compassionate voice. She explained to him what she was going to do, and why she was doing it. She told him what had happened to him, why he was attached to machines and what would happen when she disconnected them. And then she did it. For 10 minutes the three of us watched Eric being perfectly still. I'm not sure I did much breathing either. Then she told him, and probably purposely us, that she was going to turn everything back on so that his organs would be preserved and his donation could happen in the way he had requested. His chest started moving again. I have never once regretted living through those 10 minutes. It was a true goodbye time. The sun was pouring through the window continuously, which really seemed to help. Ralph and I clung to each other; I don't remember what, if anything, we said.

Lisa and Howard stayed with us long into the evening, saying little, sharing love. Howard was the fellow who located a lawyer willing to handle all the necessary paperwork. He was an empathetic lawyer and helped us answer more questions than we ever could have imagined being asked. Eric had no Will, but kept fairly comprehensive records in his computer. That helped enormously.

Ralph and I phoned our other son, Bruce, who happened to be working in Houston that week. Savannah, Georgia, is his home, but he travels around the world with the ship building business. He flew to Denver the next morning. Ralph picked him up at the airport and we met at Eric's mobile home in Boulder. The next three days were spent tearing Eric's home and history into a great many small parts. Bruce went through all the computer files — sending messages to bosses and friends, closing accounts where he could, keeping lists for the lawyer. Ralph tackled the physical files and spent time contacting mutual funds and brokers, getting death certificates and sending them out into the world. I was on serious house cleaning duty — Eric was meticulous about things which were *important*, i.e. computer connected. But he was a major slob when it came to kitchens and bathrooms.

One morning I drove back to the hospital to pick up Eric's belongings. Eric's small car seemed happy to get out of the driveway. It was a trip I wanted to do on my own. The fellows were involved with files and paperwork, the ugly rented van had already made a trip to Goodwill, and stacks were building up with items to go off in various directions to family and friends.

Nobody paid any attention to me as I walked into the ward and passed the sign which didn't say I couldn't go in, but implied the room was off limits. The organ people were due, but there was no time listed. I ended up having some totally private, quiet time telling Eric how much I appreciated the many wonderful years he'd given me. He was not in the body on the bed, though his no-longer-needed-chest was rising and falling to the rhythm of clicking pumps and graphing gadgets. But he was in the area enough to talk to, and I felt comforted. I left after about 15 minutes and picked up the plastic Patient's Belongs bag with his name printed in huge black letters. I thanked a couple of people and went away. Eric's kidneys went to two people in New York, eyes to two young people in the Denver area, bones and skin to various organ banks. He'd have been pleased: it was what he had planned.

Dave took off a couple of work days to help with the sorting. He knew which of Eric's friends needed computer components, TVs, VCRs, tapes and Eric's innumerable tools.

From the computer and paper files and our memories from letters and phone calls, we had a good start of a list of Eric's local friends. We ended up with about 50 people to notify. Ralph came up with the idea of having an old-fashioned wake. Or at least our idea of what a wake might, or ought to, be. Ralph has a long-time sailing friend who owns an Italian restaurant in Boulder. This kind fellow agreed to set up a separate room Sunday evening for our party. He couldn't make it available on Saturday. The people who had to drive back home to the south side of Denver came to the wake anyway. Work day and school be darned.

We sent invitations to friends, families, and friends of friends who had known Eric. The youngest was about eight. A year before Eric had given his extensive Lego set to this bouncy kid. We were the old crocks of the evening. One of the women is a card carrying Wiccan with True Belief written in every motion of her lithe body. During weekends she holds drumming ceremonies. She has a day job, though what it is I never learned. Eric's one time girlfriend, Minga, brought her daughter, Amy. Minga and her ex are doing a super job of raising their beautiful girl. She, as well as Lisa, has been very good about keeping in touch with us and letting us know what is happening to Eric's gang and their kids.

The party started with someone sending a puffy sympathy card and a pen around the table. Then one of the men hollered across the table asking if Dave was the guy who'd bought the piece of land in the hills near Longmont — the piece of land across the road from the acreage Eric owned. "Yes." and, "Yes." Suddenly there were voices coming from every direction telling of an adventure or meeting they'd had with Eric. They were telling each other, and us, what their connection had been with Eric. They talked about the year Eric lived in a cabin at Nederland above Boulder so he could go skiing every evening after work. They discussed the invention for which Eric received a U.S. Patent. The Down syndrome teenager showed off his new "Eric" watch which we'd passed along to him. He explained to us all that Eric had told him how it worked, and that it really did work that way. They described the trip Eric had taken driving far north in his little Honda in hopes of seeing the northern lights. A neighbor thanked us for the bright blue file cabinet and the floor lamp made out of cholla by Eric's great-grandfather. A very quiet Chinese co-worker told how Eric taught him that it is not only OK to think differently from those around you, but that it is vital if an original idea is ever to materialize. Lisa said she always ate menudo when she and Howard ate out with Eric, and that stomach lining as a meal really turned Eric off (me too). We heard about the special dish Eric always took to potluck meals: chicken enchiladas — a recipe from his pharmacist grandmother. Minga added that Eric never cooked a chicken in his whole life; he always bought a roasted one from the grocery store and used canned green chili. Correct.

And so the evening went, full of laughter, sometimes weird memories, all with explanations between the formerly unmet friends. We stayed mostly quiet and tried to take in all the stories and obvious fondness for the fellow with whom they had all spent special time. The Wiccan gal assured us that he was with us and enjoying the stories. We all hoped so. It was a most wondrous wake.

Since Eric died, I've met many women, and several men, who

have lost a child. Each has reacted to his tragedy in his own way, and I have grown stronger in the sharing of even the outer most layer of their anguish. I discovered that Eric had an extremely strong support group during the years after he left home. I have finally realized how truly vital those friendships, assistance, and intercommunication are to my own physical and mental health. From each side, I've seen that a gentle word or a soft touch can help heal the totally unbearable.

Dear Friend Jenny
by
Dorothy Hendryx Kollman

My mother, Elva Hendryx, and Jenny Sheaver were friends before I was born. Mother often took me to see Jenny. So it was natural for me, as I grew up, to consider her my friend too.

Our home was on the edge of Center Point, Iowa, and Jenny's medium sized farm only a quarter of a mile away. When I was about 6, I was allowed to walk there by myself.

She had milk cows, pigs, chickens, geese, turkeys, guinea hens and bantam chickens. When a calf was born, in order to get it to suckle, she taught me to first put my hand in the warm milk; then next, put my finger in the calf's mouth, drawing it to the mother's udder. How proud I was when I accomplished that! When we fed the pigs, it was a feeding frenzy — they lack good table manners. When the sows gave birth in the spring, they could have as many as 12 to 14 piglets.

Jenny kept about 50 to 100 chickens year round. In the spring she bought baby chicks from the local hatchery. She taught me how to feed them corn by broadcasting it on the ground. We also gave them chicken grit (finely ground stone) to make the corn digestible. When I was tall enough to reach the nests I helped gather the eggs. She taught me to reach under the hen with my palm up to avoid being painfully pecked too often. You very carefully put the egg in your hand, pulled it back slowly and put it in a basket. These lady chickens laid so many eggs that Center Point residents came to the farm to buy them.

The geese and banty roosters were somehow to be avoided. The geese would run after me, wings flapping, preparing to knock me down. The banties would hide and when I approached them they would jump out and nip my ankles very painfully.

These are some of the things she taught me in her patient and gentle way. I learned to listen, follow instructions and feel proud of myself for helping Jenny.

Every spring Jenny planted a huge garden. We eagerly watched for the seeds to germinate and the sprouts to pop out of the ground. Each time I visited her during growing season, we had a tour of the garden. She often sent me home with a bag of vegetables. She particularly loved flowers, as I did. The flower garden was a riot of color. Many times she sent a bouquet of flowers for my mother. I learned to love the soil and what it produced.

Jenny's husband, Archie, was a bee keeper. He tended several bee hives. He made us laugh when he put on his protective gear. One day he decided to put this gear on me. The gear included a hat, a fine mesh veil (so I could see the bees, but they could not sting my face), and a heavy coverup that went down to my knees and tied at the waist — all one piece. Last but not least, he put on me his bee keeper gloves that came up to my elbows. Of course, looking at this little girl dressed in this oversized bee keeper's garb produced lots of laughter from onlookers. Lesson learned — it's OK to laugh at yourself.

I had a huge fascination with the windmill in Jenny's backyard. There was nothing better on a hot summer afternoon than a drink of cold water pumped up into a tin cup.

Also, there was an outbuilding where the cream was separated from the milk. The electric cream separator was a fairly large piece of equipment. After the separation was complete, the milk cans were picked up by the dairy truck and taken to the plant to be processed and sold. The electric cream separator had to be immaculately cleaned for use the next day. When I was about 8 years old Jenny suggested I clean the equipment, under her supervision. After watching her do this many, many times I felt confident and did it to her satisfaction. I was one proud little girl when Jenny complimented me on my good work.

The only magazines available to me were at Jenny's. My favorite was the National Geographic. Those stories and photos stirred the imagination of a young girl from a small town in Iowa who had never been more than 20 miles from home. I looked at the magazines during "rest time" and Jenny and I talked about the faraway places with strange sounding names. Because of those talks, I visited some of the places later.

It wasn't all work at my friend Jenny's house. We often had tea parties, but best of all was the Christmas party. We had Christmas cookies, gift exchange and wonder of wonders a play written by Dorothy Hendryx (me). My little brother Duane was invited for this event. He and I were always the supporting cast to Jenny. She played her dramatic role with flair. We had so much fun.

I always had to ask Mother if I could stay late to help Jenny bring the milk cows from the pasture to the barn. For both of us, this was our favorite chore at the best part of the day. Jenny carried a tall walking stick to keep the cows in line. After the cows were in their stalls Jenny would give me a big hug and I would start my way home thinking about all the events of the day.

Dear friend Jenny was soft spoken, patient, smart, loving and above all, caring. At this time of my life I still frequently think of her, my mentor.

Betty
by
Dorothy Losee

Nearly all of us have someone who consciously or unconsciously influences our lives. I was fortunate enough to have my aunt, Betty Blanchard. She was the much loved youngest of five sisters, a 'bonus baby" we would say today, as her mother was 41 when she was born. Her sisters were Dorothy (I'm her name sake), Helen (my mother), Charlotte and Harriett. Sadly, the  girls lost their mother, a victim of tuberculosis, two years after Betty was born — something all too common in the cold climes of northern Minnesota.

The first year after her mother's death Dorothy, the eldest, stayed home from college to help her father cope with his loss and help with the younger sisters. The next year, my mother, Helen, left Parsons School of Design in New York to do the same thing. My grandfather felt he could not manage a household with two little girls, so Betty (age 4) and Harriett (age 9) were sent to Villa Maria Academy, a Catholic boarding school just ten miles from home. Here Betty, a sunny happy little girl with beautiful red curls, lived for 12 years, graduating valedictorian of her class.

I was her proud wreath bearer at the ceremony.

Secretarial school followed, but just after her 17th birthday, she contracted tuberculosis. For five long years she lived in the sanitarium. Did she complain? Not once. Instead she became self-educated: learning from those around her, reading vociferously and emerging with a greater spectrum of knowledge than many college graduates.

After two illness-free years, she again became ill with TB and had surgery to collapse her lung. The incision stretched from her shoulder across her back to her lower rib cage. When she recovered, she was hired as Mrs. Fowler McCormick's confidential secretary — a wonderful job. The McCormicks owned beautiful homes in Illinois, Arizona and Florida. Betty lived in all of them.

Following another short bout of TB, she and my mother sailed for Europe to visit their sister, Charlotte. She was living in Germany with her husband, Colonel Raymond Rule, who was involved in the Nuremberg trials. My mother returned home at the end of the summer, but Betty stayed on for a year. She traveled alone or with Charlotte to every place she had always dreamed of seeing.

My father had died several years before and Mother had moved to California to be near cousins she was very fond of. She had purchased a new home and on her return from Europe, Betty joined her. What a happy time that was! Betty was working as a legal secretary in Santa Monica. Betty was so funny. For instance, Mother loved to shop at the Farmers' Market and Betty would say, "Let's go to the Marmers' Farket," or "Helen, it's time to get our shu flots?" When she visited me in New Mexico and ate a quesadilla with salsa for the first time, she described it as "a lighted match between two pieces of cardboard!" — but she did eventually develop a love for Mexican food.

People loved to be around her. I loved to be around her. She and Mother would come from California to New Mexico to stay with our children when my husband and I travelled. They adored her and called her Auntie B.

Betty's run with poor health never ceased. She had breast cancer which resulted in a double mastectomy. Her body was ravaged with scars but it didn't faze her. She always looked lovely. When her medical doctor asked her to allow him to illustrate the results of his surgical techniques to doctors at medical meetings, she agreed and jokingly asked how she should comport herself from her wheelchair. "Should I look coyly over my shoulder at the audience or just be serious about the whole thing?"

When my girls were 7 and 4, Betty came to spend Christmas with us. Though she tried her best to keep up her sense of humor and happy outlook, she wasn't herself. Soon afterward she was diagnosed with abdominal cancer. She lived four more months. Like her mother, she died at age 43.

Betty taught me to accept whatever happens without whining or complaining. I have tried to follow her example through my life. My husband and I (both only children) faced the loss of his mother and my father within a year and a half after we married. We lost a long-awaited baby when I had to undergo surgery for an ovarian tumor and I was stricken with polio as the mother of a beautiful 10-month-old baby girl. I was in the hospital, then in therapy and on crutches for many weeks. When our second daughter was born two years later, I was fine — thanks to my wonderful husband who saw to it that I never missed an exercise session. I persevered with optimism. "I will have to get over it and I will." I had Betty as my shining example. If she could do it, I could do it.

To this day I have continued to face challenges. Ten years ago I had surgery for breast cancer and have fully recovered. For six years I've had macular degeneration. When I could no longer read with regular glasses, I got special magnifying glasses and then a video eye to enlarge printing onto a screen. I tell myself today that not recognizing people's faces is a small thing when compared to those who have lost their sight entirely. Betty would say, "Lucky girl." and I agree.

What Comes Next?
by
Virginia "Ginna" Strike Malone

Here I am in the middle of a big move…again!

"Big move?" you say. "Just around the corner? That's not big."

Yeah, for me it is. I'm in the stage of unpack, put away, then can't find again. Yeah, for me now, it's pretty big.

So how do I have the time to listen to you urging me to write about some person, place, or event that had a significant influence in my life? Just
one?…in five pages or less….can I do that? So many people, so many places and events. But wait, this may be exciting. Let's see. If I chose a person it would have to be my mother, but that's a book I've already written — confusing, difficult, full of love and pain, and joy and change. A place? No, too many of those for one to stand out.

An event? — ah, not one, but many. I think all those moves Mother made when I was growing up definitely influenced who I became. My mother — a grieving widow, running away from sorrow, chasing happiness — moved us from one place to another. And even after she remarried we went back and forth to the ranch every summer and most holidays. Then there were the places where I stayed in town to go to school, while Mother went to the ranch to take care of my stepdad. Lots of places; lots of moves. Even before we left Pasadena the first time, I think I can count six or seven houses where we lived.

"Honey, we've only got this much space left for the rest of your toys in the big box Uncle Lee got. See. There's room for the roller skates, but not the shells and rocks from the beach."

"But the shells are so pretty and they smell like the ocean. You said they don't have an ocean where we're going."

"They'll get all smelly and faded. You'll like the roller skates best. We'll take them. You'll love Texas. We'll be happy there with my family and lots of cousins for you to play with. You won't miss the beach."

"Aunt Alfa and Uncle Lee are family."

Oh, this will be better for my sweet little girl."

"But…."

"Come on, we need to hurry and finish this packing."

But we didn't get to Texas then. We stayed in New Mexico that year, then Texas. And a year after that we moved again, back to California.

Is there any wonder that special "things" became so precious to me? In addition to that familiar thing left behind, there were the cherished memories attached to each one. I didn't want to forget who gave them to me or what was happening when I got them.

There were good things and bad things about each move, each new place.

One good thing I learned was how to make new friends — but then again, I didn't find out how to stay in a friendship and fight and make up over and over again. We moved before I could do that. No siblings, no long term friends until I got to junior high — most of them I got to keep and some I still have. But I've had to teach myself how to disagree with my friend and not threaten our friendship. Occasionally, I still get worried when I disagree — that person might not want me as a friend any longer. I want to keep my friends — not lose them, or move away as I had to do all those times before.

"Oh, darling, I've just decided for sure that we're moving back to California. We'll plan to get on the train about a month after school is out. That ought to give us time to get all our packing done."

"You mean leave here — everybody here — all the cousins?"

"It will be better and healthier out there. Those awful mumps were terrible for both of us."

"Will we live close to the beach, Mother?"

"Close enough."

They say all the early childhood habits are hard to change. It can be done — and to great advantage — but the old habits lurk as the default position. Learning new things that you missed learning at the appropriate time can be awkward. It's like being a teenager at 50. Teenagers are expected to be clumsy, to have wild passions one week and not the next — like purple and red hair, or expecting to become a rock star. We older people may seem ridiculous and awkward trying new things like adopting a gallery of stuffed animals — you should see mine, but you can't have my teddy bear or my rabbit, either. But I hope we can still stay friends even when I'm silly or forgetful, because friends are precious to me.

Another thing happened as we went from place to place. I got to see the world from the "other side of the mountain." I had a new "world view" in every new town. The kids at school were different. The culture was different.

In California they liked beaches and parks and going to plays. Cities have so much to do — so many new things to learn. We went to museums and concerts, but in some houses there were no kids next door. Practicing to perform as "living statues" in the summer festival at the park gave the little kids from around Pasadena time to play together, while we waited for the big kids to do their thing.

In that really small town in Texas surrounded by farms, my cousins and I climbed pecan trees and wandered around my uncle's farm. One time I ditched my younger girl cousin to sneak back with my older boy cousins and take one of Uncle Otto's watermelons, break it open and eat it right out in the field. That was fun. But Uncle Otto got mad. We had to take responsibility for what we did. Everybody knew what everyone else did.

In New Mexico they liked going to the movie on Saturday morning to see the serials. We played cowboys and Indians — and Red Rover, Come Over. I got my first bicycle in New Mexico. We made our own fun — did things for ourselves. In high school, we went to dances every Friday night at the Women's Club. At college in California we often went out and sat to watch performances. When I went to new places I knew to watch carefully and find out the customs and beliefs in that place in order to figure out how I might fit in. And those beliefs affect so much of what we do.

By the time I graduated and got married, life on the farm beckoned as a haven of stability. I enjoyed raising my kids, doing housewifely things, and expecting to stay in one place for the rest of my life. My husband remained alive for only 22 years. It was the longest time I'd lived in one place.

As a young child I had no choice in moving, but the habit must have become a part of me. I liked seeing new places, facing new challenges, learning new things. I've always been curious about most everything. So when my husband died and my kids were in college, it was easy to make the next big change — leave the farm and go to graduate school in Albuquerque. Those experiences of change from traveling around as a kid made later life-style changes "normal behavior."

Next came life as a working woman (I loved being a psychologist.) Then came a second marriage to an author — another new life full of different and exciting experiences. I am lucky to have had so many lifetimes in this one I've been allotted. I cherish what I have learned regardless of the struggle the lessons may have been. I'm glad I know why it's hard to part with those stuffed animals, to hold my friends close even when we get crossways, and how much a different viewpoint can effect a person's beliefs and behavior. So here I am in La Vida Llena and moving to a new apartment. I hope that means I'm still capable of making changes. But I don't want to move again.

At times in the past, I prayed to never lose the ability to learn and grow — I don't mean physically around the middle, though I did; but in my mind, my emotions, psyche, behavior and spirit. Well, the challenges keep coming. They are interesting and sometimes I even seek them out (will I ever master this computer or the spelling for texting? RUlistening?) But more often now I get weary, so maybe I could rest today. Yes, I get tired, but I think I'd get more tired just sitting with nothing interesting to do, nothing to learn, no new people to meet. I'm lucky to live here. Even now I learn new things about the friends of a lifetime. People are endlessly fascinating, don't you think?

Mrs. McGillicuddy, Where Are You?!
by
Renee Mazon

When I was 6 years of age and lived in New York City, my parents told me that they had a special treat for me. One Sunday afternoon we drove a very long way and finally arrived at a farm. It was very exciting because they had animals, chickens, ducks and little babies of each kind. I could play with them. I saw a woman milk a cow and realized that not all milk came out of bottles. I was al-

lowed to feed the chickens. I threw their food on the ground and they all ran after it, flapping their wings and making a racket. I squealed with delight. We spent a long time there and I couldn't have been happier.

Just before we were going to leave, the farmer took me into the barn, picked up a chicken which he put on a tree stump, grabbed an axe and chopped its head off. The body was flapping around on the ground while the head was somewhere else. It was bleeding. I started to scream and tried to put the head back on the body. The farmer laughed and said he was going to eat the chicken for dinner. I had blood all over my hands and clothes and I was still crying. I was very frightened of the farmer because I was afraid he would do that to me. I ran out of the barn. He took me back to my parents who washed me up and took me home.

I cried all the way home as I hid on the floor of the back seat of the car. I had never thought about where the food I ate came from; but I never ate chicken again until I was an adult.

It was 1939. I was 10 years old. Every Saturday afternoon, my friends and I would go to the kiddie matinees at the Uptown Movie Theatre. For 10 cents per kid, our families would be able to enjoy some adult time at home, while the children were watching a movie, a serial, a coming attraction and a newsreel.

As I was watching the newsreel, I saw a bunch of strange looking objects all thrown together in a very big hole. I found it scary and I kept staring at it. After looking more closely I realized, to my horror, that they looked like very skinny, naked dead people that were piled on top of one another. The word "JEWS" kept flashing on the screen. It frightened me so much that I ran out of the auditorium and went into the ladies' room and cried. When my friends were getting ready to leave, they realized that I wasn't there; so, they looked in the ladies' room and found me crying and shaking. They took me home.

I told my mother about the skinny dead people in the big hole. She said that in a far off country called Germany, bad people called Nazis, were killing Jews. I asked her what Jews were. She said WE were Jews. I didn't know what Jews were or that I was one — but I was afraid I would be like those bones in that big hole. She assured me that we lived in America and that could never happen to us. Once, some cousins came to visit us. They had escaped from Nazi Germany and told us horrific stories about the Holocaust.

Somehow, in my young mind, I connected both these violent incidents. I vowed never to harm anything or anyone — or engage in violence of any kind. I am 82 years old now and can still see, in intricate details, those two violent experiences.

In high school I was frequently an honor student, but kept

failing Modern History due to the fact that I refused to attend the classes. The class material was about all the wars, their dates and the reasons for them.

As an adult I became a member of the American Society of Friends, also known as Quakers. They are pacifists — will not bear arms in any war, but will work as ambulance drivers, hospital workers and clerical personnel during wartime. The Quakers are concerned with non-violence in a variety of ways. They frequently have workshops about how to release the violent feelings within themselves.

It was during one of those workshops that I learned there was not only physical violence, but there was emotional violence, as well — which in my opinion, is far more damaging. When Quaker Meetings were not available to me, I became a Buddhist or a Unitarian depending on which one was available. All of them stress non-violence and respect for all others. They have been my religions of choice all my adult life. I am a member of the Unitarian church, today.

Interestingly, I have never been able to accept Judaism as my religion, although I have made several attempts to do so. I consider myself a secular Jew because according to Jewish law, if my mother was Jewish, then I am Jewish. I do enjoy Jewish music, food and humor. I have a huge collection of Jewish music and am very proud of the contributions that my small group of people have made to the scientific, medical, intellectual, financial, musical and theatrical worlds — to name just a few.

However, the Jewish religion as I knew it, was very inhospitable to women. Women were considered unclean, second class citizens and not privy to higher education. I am delighted to say that this has changed greatly since the liberal modern movements (Conservative, Reconstructionist and Reformed) have been established and grown. In these movements, women are now equal with men. Many women are returning to Judaism and being very active in the synagogues.

I was a very sensitive child. It presented quite a challenge to my parents. I did not share their values, interests or attitudes. I would fantasize that the stork, who delivered babies, made a mistake when she was delivering me. She dropped me off at Mrs. Birnbaum's house instead of where I really belonged — at Mrs. McGillicuddy's house.

They Gave Me the Gift of Music
by
Josephine D. "Jo" Mechem

The person, actually two people, who most influenced my life were my mother and father, Helen and Wallace Donavan.

In 1928-1929 my parents moved their three children and Grandma to five acres (nearly a city block). The property had a small house, a huge two story barn and another small building that was later used to raise turkeys and chickens. It was a mile from the University Park grade school which was at the end of the streetcar line and close to the University of Denver.

These two wonderful people were dealing with the start of the Great Depression. Dad was a small contractor. He learned his trade by taking care of his parents' rental property at 17th and Broadway near downtown Denver. He also gained experience and crafts-manship when he remodeled and did extensive repair work at my grandfather's ranch in Arkansas, so that his dad could put the ranch on the market to sell. He was in high demand with plenty of work during my childhood.

Much of his "pay" was in trade and barter as that was a way of life in those days. One fine fall day a beautiful seven foot grand piano was delivered to our home. It took up nearly half of the living room! Dad had remodeled a music store and that piano was part of the payment.

Taking up another chunk of the living room was an upright electric player piano. My brother, sister and I would lock the keys, turn it on and pretend we were playing for anyone visiting. However, there was a truly accomplished musician in our home and that was my mother. She and a good friend were practicing duet piano pieces as often as chores and children would allow. They played for many of the important events in South Denver. The true beauty of the pianos and Mother's playing was the music that was continuously in our home.

As each of my siblings and I entered junior high we were given the opportunity to choose an instrument from a large inventory owned by the Denver schools. My sister, who was tall, chose a string bass, my brother a tuba and I chose a cello. Our junior high music teacher, Arthur E. Cage, could play all of the instruments a little, so he helped us get started.

When Dad repaired a porch for the Denver Symphony 1st chair bass player, part of the payment was a year of lessons for my sister, Helen. Dad painted the music store and I got a wooden cello to replace the metal one on loan from my school. What a difference that made! It brought new dimensions of beauty to my playing.

My parents saw to it that all three of us attended all our rehearsals. They drove a car loaded with instruments and kids to and from rehearsals, concerts and lessons all over Denver. These two fabulous people made sure we had all that was necessary to compete for positions in the different orchestras in town. By the time we were in high school they were chauffeuring us to the Antonio Bricos All Women Orchestra and the Denver University Orchestra.

I'm not sure how they got us to practice. Perhaps it was by example and praise — watching Mama practice while Dad rocked in his favorite rocking chair, read, and encouraged her and each of us. If we begged he would play the Cherry Street Rag which was all the rage in the 1930s.

Mother and I rode the street car to meet the conductor of the Junior Symphony and ask when the auditions would be held and what he expected from youth who became part of this ensemble. Again, when all of us were accepted, the cars were full of kids and instruments for the rehearsals and concerts. It was quite a feat when the Junior Symphony was chosen to help test the sound system being installed in the fantastic 10,000-seat Red Rocks Amphitheater in the foothills west of Denver. Summer concerts are still held there.

My parents also were involved with their bridge club, friends and cookouts. Mother's hard work made our lovely flower gardens, thick grass and tall shade trees the favorite choice for summer parties. From November to March they regularly took us to ice skate after dinner at Washington Park Lake, if we hurried and got the dinner dishes done. They still had their own lives and work to manage, yet everything seemed to get done and as always, music came first. As I look back, I so treasure these two wonderful devoted parents who were ever present with encouragement, help, willingness to volunteer and setting a fine example in their own daily lives.

They gave me the gift of music and cello that accompanied me into and throughout my adult life. When I moved to New Mexico as a new bride, the cello enabled me to quickly blend into the community by playing with the Albuquerque Civic Orchestra. As it evolved into the New Mexico Symphony Orchestra, so did I — I played with them for over 25 years. My parents gave me a wonderful opportunity and I thank them each and every day for the gift of music.

A Slice in Time
by
Ruth Shore Mondlick

In 1963, spellbound, I watched my husband of 14 years take my most prized possession, my world literature text book, and slash it with a razor.

Labor Day, 10 years earlier: I had been ill for several days with muscle aches and nausea that I attributed to a particularly nasty case of the flu. After I settled my 22-month-old son into his crib for his nap, I became so ill that my husband, Martin, called our family doctor. One house call later, my husband rushed me to the hospital. I was 22 years old and five months pregnant. I had a husband. I had a toddler. And I had polio.

The next days and weeks are a blur. One minute I walked into our car, and the next minute I was completely paralyzed from the neck down, unable to so much as scratch my nose.

Gradually, the practical issues were sorted out: Yes, I would live; no to an abortion; yes to moving me from Providence to Boston Children's Hospital, a teaching hospital for Harvard Medical School, where they routinely cared for the more serious cases. The future was uncertain. Martin found a woman to care for our son. Although we did not know it then, it would be six and a half months, some of it spent in an iron lung, before I would return home.

I was placed in a ward with three other women. One had given birth to her daughter a few weeks before her diagnosis. We were told that pregnant women were particularly susceptible to the poliovirus. The company of the other women was as important to our recovery as the physical therapy. I imagine it was like sharing a foxhole, except that our enemy was the poliovirus.

No pain medications were allowed. The only relief we had from the pain of muscle spasms was the hot packs developed by Sister Elizabeth Kenny. The hot packs were pieces of woolen blankets wrung out of boiling water. At Boston Children's the blankets were wrung out in the spin cycle of washing machines rolled to bedsides. I still cringe at the smell of wet wool.

Physical therapists worked with each of us twice daily, painfully stretching unused muscles and coaxing them to move, however faintly. When breathing became too difficult, the doctors placed me in an iron lung. With the exception of my head and neck, every part of me was enclosed in an airtight, cylindrical steel drum. Although confining, it was a relief to feel the periodic increase and decrease of pressure on my chest taking in and expelling air as the sealed, airtight compartment did the work of breathing for me.

Mine was not the only grueling schedule. Martin had breakfast with our little boy every morning before leaving for his law office. After a full day of work, he would hop a train from our home in Providence, Rhode Island, for the hour and a half ride to Boston. From the train station, he took a subway to Boston Children's to visit with me. I don't know when he ate dinner. I don't know what time he finally arrived home. He kept to this schedule six days a week the entire time I was in the hospital.

On February 3, 1954, I gave birth to a healthy seven pound three ounce baby boy. We were elated. A month and a half later, I returned home.

Those first few months at home were the most frustrating. It was at home that my limitations hit me full force. The residual weakness of polio left me with a useless left arm and hand, a modestly functioning right arm, and weakened legs. I could not care for my family. I had all I could do to care for myself.

My doctor at Boston Children's Hospital did not trust physical therapists who were not under his direct supervision. He preferred to train relatives to give physical therapy to his discharged patients. Consequently, Martin became my physical therapist — two sessions, seven days a week for several years.

Together, day after day and year after year, we worked towards our mutual goal: that I care for myself and my family independent of outside help.

Together, we achieved that goal. But gradually, I wanted more. I had been engaged to Martin at 17 and married at 18. I worked while Martin completed Harvard Law School, and our first child arrived fairly quickly after that. Then polio and another baby. There had been no time for college.

In 1963, ten years after the onset of polio, both children were in elementary school. We were living in Miami Shores, Florida, and I craved a college education. My time had come. I filled out applications, sent for transcripts, took test after test after test, and I was accepted at Barry College, a small liberal arts college just fifteen minutes from our home. I would be able to take classes while the boys were in school and be home in plenty of time to care for them. Polio had postponed college. It had not stolen my dream.

I breezed through registration and left the college book store elated with my two text books: *A Survey of World Literature* and *A Survey of Western Civilization*. They were big, heavy books. Too big and too heavy. My legs had improved greatly, but neither arm would ever fully recover. As I walked from the book store to my car, I dropped my books every couple of feet. Finally, a fellow student picked them up and walked me to my car.

When Martin returned from work that evening, he found a

tearful wife. "I can't go to college," I said. "I can't carry the text-books."

Martin said nothing. He calmly walked into the other room and returned with a straight-edged razor. He sliced my books into chapters so that I could carry a chapter at a time to class.

That act changed my life. It opened my world. We moved to Albuquerque, New Mexico, in 1964 where I continued my education and earned a B.A. with a major in English and a minor in Philosophy at the University of New Mexico (UNM). I taught at Sandia Preparatory School for several years. After that, I earned my Ph.D. in Counseling Psychology at UNM and became a licensed psychologist.

I went on to a challenging, satisfying career in Psychology, both as a clinician and as a Clinical Assistant Professor in the Department of Psychiatry at the UNM Medical School. In 1988 I was appointed to the New Mexico Board of Psychologist Examiners for a three year term.

My life changed forever and for the better, because of one small act — and a sharp razor.

Jeanne's New Life
by
Jeanne Moore

"Today is the day," I thought as we headed for northern New Mexico. It was September 1970 and our destination was Ghost Ranch, the Presbyterian Conference grounds. My husband, Moe, and I had been there many times since we had moved to New Mexico in 1958. The location had wonderful memories of annual family camps, couples' retreats and church led gatherings. But somehow this time was different.

Even though I was co-chairman of the weekend, the program was in the hands of a group from the Methodist Lay Witness Mission. Their plans were a mystery to me and anticipation was high for the spiritual impact ahead.

For some time Moe and I had been dissatisfied with our church and it's lukewarm impact on our lives. Since 1968 when Young Life, a para-church ministry to high schoolers, had sponsored leaders in Albuquerque, we had seen dramatic positive changes in our three teenage sons when they attended Young Life meetings twice a week. They had an enthusiasm about God and Jesus that was infectious. Because communist youth groups were springing up across the

U.S. at that time, we had investigated Young Life to be sure it was a legitimate Christian organization. Our investigation provided the information we needed to encourage our sons to be active in Young Life.

Being interested and available parents, we started chaperoning weekend retreats at Young Life camps in Colorado. This gave us first hand experiences with the Young Life leaders and their sincere love and concern for teens and their relationship with God — but what about adults?

We had heard about the Methodist Lay Witness program for adults and as we became acquainted with their leaders, we sensed the same Godly love and direction in their lives that Young Life people had. This is how our weekend came together and over 60 friends from our church were ready to learn more.

Our Ghost Ranch weekend was wonderful! Enthusiastic singing and small group sharing bonded us in a new way to our fellow church members and old friends. At our closing meeting, Moe and I were in the front row and we observed a row of empty chairs facing us. Our curiosity was aroused and we wondered who would be seated facing us. The closing song, "Just as I Am," was starting the second chorus and the invitation "to change my life" was extended. I prayed and knew that this change was the answer to the emptiness and need I'd been feeling. I responded to the opportunity being offered. It was as if a giant hand on my back gently moved me forward and I kneeled at a chair facing me. Moe was moving at the same time and also kneeled — and we were not kneelers! The Holy Spirit had drawn us, as one, to surrender our hearts to Jesus Christ our Savior. His joy and forgiveness filled our hearts and cleansing tears flowed. Moe hadn't cried since he was a child. As time passed and prayers flowed from our hearts, we were totally unaware of our surroundings or other people in the room. Only God was there and He was our All in All.

When we finally stood and looked around, the same thing had

happened to all of the others in the room. It was like in the book of Acts when the Holy Spirit fell on all the people in the upper room. Now we understood what had happened to our sons. We were experiencing the new life as we were "born again."

What a thrilling time was had by all present at lunch that day! Each person was amazed at the change that had supernaturally come over the group. We were sharing the need for prayers to keep that fire in our hearts alive. We'd experienced the "Ghost Ranch high" at other times and didn't want this fresh relationship with God to vanish as it had before when we returned to Albuquerque.

The days that followed in Albuquerque were like a honeymoon with God. My big surprise was on Tuesday. I was in the shower when Moe stuck his head in and asked if we could host a prayer meeting at our home on Wednesday night. That was totally out of character for him and he explained that the men had been on the phone making plans to gather for prayer and Bible study. That was the first evidence of change to a new life centered in the Lord and His word and in fellowship with other believers.

The harmony in our home was so unique as we shared the love and dedication to God that our sons had already. That atmosphere was attracting many teens to our home on a daily basis, so we began a weekly Saturday night activity for youth. We had punch, cookies, Christian music, games and sharing for the 25 to 50 kids who joined in the fun. The word passed around quickly and our youth outreach continued for over three years. Moe worked Saturday nights and I really enjoyed the teens and their craziness.

Our daughter also was led into Christ's loving arms, but turned away when she was 14. We still loved her and after she was 35 she rededicated her life to God. All three sons and their wives and most of my 15 grandchildren are believers and are serving God with their gifts.

My life has been so impacted by my faith and dedication to God. I've had the usual life issues with family members, including terminal illness, death and drugs. In each situation He has strengthened me, given me the wisdom needed and always been at my side. I continue to praise Him for the unity in my family, the grace He shows as I make mistakes, and the blessings and peace He brings to my life. I've learned that external changes aren't the answer to many of my needs. God points out internal changes I need to make and provides the Holy Spirit's power for me to be the person He wants me to be.

Orders to Japan: 1948
by
Irene Myers

Going to Japan sounded exciting to me after having grown up in Philadelphia and spending weekends and vacations on the Jersey shore — that was the East Coast and the Atlantic Ocean. Now I would be traveling to the West Coast and crossing the Pacific Ocean to live in Japan for several years. Little did I know what a life-changing experience this would be — so many events and scenes heightened by understanding the working class Japanese fishermen and farmers.

We wanted to have our Studebaker in Japan, so we drove from Aberdeen Proving Ground, Maryland, to San Francisco. Our trip was without incident except for a snowstorm which delayed us for three days in North Platt, Nebraska. I still wonder why our TripTik routed us the northern route in the winter. But we did make it to San Francisco in good time for my husband, Charles, to board the Army transport.

My little 2-year-old daughter, Irene, and I spent three months living in a small apartment in Rodeo, California, awaiting our call to sail out of San Francisco to Japan. Since I was pregnant, I couldn't do many active things. I read so many stories to Irene that she could tell me the story just by looking at a page.

The Army transport we boarded was crowded with many mothers-to-be and many children. One of the officers on board talked to Irene on deck one day and she told him in no uncertain terms she was going to Japan to see her Daddy. So was everybody else, but she wanted to emphasize that SHE was going to Japan.

The highlight of the trip was a party for all the children having a birthday that month. It took us 23 days to cross the ocean and there were many birthdays during that time. All the children were invited. It was a big affair with ice cream and cake, and balloons. Irene was turning 3 years old.

Irene and I stood on deck and watched a pale gray line on the horizon. This gray line became larger and out of it grew a mountain, Mt. Fuji, and then we saw the shore line. The next thing we knew we were docking at Yokohama. Charles was there to greet us. There were lots of husbands in uniform waiting to greet their families and take them to the train station. I thought I was going to faint from the odor. I don't know if it was from smelling fish or so many people in one place, but I found it hard to find my breath. Perhaps it was partly due to my being seven months pregnant. Japanese trains are for shorter people than Americans and I completely filled a berth. When I found I couldn't move, I started to laugh. I laughed all the way to Kobe. The scenery was beautiful with lush green fields and terracing on the hills. The workers were laboring well past sunset.

Our house in Rocco Heights (military housing for Kobe) was most adequate. It was a two-story, three-bedroom home with nice furniture. Charles had been to a bingo game at the Officers' Club and won a "chow" table (coffee table) which had a lovely scene inlaid with ivory — a most welcoming addition.

One day I was looking out the window, taking in the scene of Kobe harbor. There were ships and ocean-going vessels from all over the world. There were Chinese junks, Japanese sampans, and

Argentinian oil tankers. I stood in amazement watching all of this international traffic happening in the harbor. My world view was certainly broadening — never to be the same!

In April I went to the Army hospital in Osaka to await the birth of my second child. Phyllis was born in May and we moved to our new home on the island of Etta Jima. We had a beautiful three-bedroom house overlooking a landscaped park and the exquisite Etta Jima Bay (sunsets over Etta Jima Bay were the stuff photographers dream about). I had quite a reunion with Irene. Our maid, Sachiko, had been taking care of Irene in my absence and she and Irene had become very good friends. Sachiko's father was a ferry boat captain and she had a good education. Irene knew numbers one to ten in Japanese and Chinese and a host of little Japanese songs — thanks to Sachiko's patience with her.

We settled down to a very pleasant life. The Japanese maids, Sachiko and Yoshia, took care of the household and helped me with the children. Tannimoto did the gardening and washed the car. I did most of the cooking, but I always had one of the maids make the rice. And, Yoshia made wonderful cookies. Irene always got a chair and stood right next to her while she made the cookie dough and had a very fast finger for tasting.

We gradually became more and more acclimated to the Japanese way of life and language. To this day I find myself using Japanese words to express certain things — "chow" table for coffee table, numbers in Japanese, Japanese exclamations of surprise or pain. My terms of expression have been forever enriched by my opportunity to be immersed in the Japanese language and culture.

Our house was on the grounds of what had been the Japanese navy training center. It was surrounded by rural Japan — farming and fishing villages. Day in and day out I observed the industrious Japanese people making the very most of what little they had. We often went sunbathing and swimming on Ohara Beach (another good setting for photography). One day, as we crossed a sweet potato field on our way to the beach, we saw a young woman hoeing. When I looked in the basket beside her, there was a newborn baby. And the young woman kept right on hoeing. There were many octopuses in the water at the beach. Our lifeguard kept them at bay by putting a row of pots where the water was six feet deep. Then when the octopuses would crawl in the pots, he would collect them and, knowing they were a delicacy to the Japanese, he gave them to the local families to eat. That was a much better solution than having them cling around our ankles!

These observations and experiences of Japanese life deepened my admiration for the Japanese and forever increased my appreciation for our easier American way of life — never to be taken for granted.

One Sunday we drove to Hiroshima. The road was filled with potholes from the atom bomb being dropped there. The building at the center of the impact was a gnarled piece of steel sticking grotesquely into the sky. There were signs saying, "No More Hiroshima," to which we replied, "No more Pearl Harbor." It was the children who paid such a huge price. A group of women from the Officers' Wives' Club collected fruit and toys for children who lost their parents in the blast. They were in an orphanage and were so pitiful. For many nights I couldn't sleep for thinking about them — my heart bled for them. Seeing the consequences of war on these children magnified my feelings that war is horrible and needless.

I took Ikabana, the Japanese art of flower arranging, while in Japan. Mama-San brought flowers and branches to my home. My friend came over and Mama-San taught us to make flower arrangements so we could have fresh flower arrangements for the week. Mama-San was keeping a record of our lessons and when we had enough lessons to qualify, she asked her Yokohama office to issue diplomas for us. I still arrange flowers whenever I can.

This brings me to mention one more example of how living in Japan changed my life. We used scrip — no American money (dollars or coins) was allowed. We used scrip in the Post Exchange and Commissary and at the Officers' Club. We bought Japanese yen to spend in the local shops. But since we were in the British prescinct, we used pounds and pence when shopping on the mainland. The most confusing was our American scrip. More than once I confused a five dollar bill with a nickel. It was a relief to return to the U.S. and use American money. I never complain about counting money.

We had made many good friends and our living was so enjoyable, we weren't so anxious to leave when orders came for stateside. But the day came when we had to say, "Goodbye." Two Army transports were departing from Yokohama the same day and we were hoping for the one that would stop in Hawaii. However, we left on the one stopping in Okinawa. It turned out to be wonderful. We spent several days basking on the beautiful beaches and our three little girls collected lovely shells. And so, on to San Francisco where our first stop was the Milk Bar for our first fresh milk in years!

All Girls Should Be So Lucky
by
Maryann Nordyke

Bill Nordyke, my husband, has had the most significant influence in my life. I shall try to explain how by sharing a number of incidents in our lives.

Bill and I can't remember when we didn't know one another. We were both born and grew up in Indianapolis, Indiana. Our families were not intimate friends, but knew one another. My mother played bridge with his Aunt Nora. In the eighth grade we both joined Mrs. Gates' ballroom dancing class where the boys were required to wear white gloves so they wouldn't soil our gowns. The girls sat on one side of the room, the boys on the other, until Mrs. Gates said, "Young men, you may choose a partner." We girls waited patiently to be asked to dance. It was at this time I got to know Bill much better. During this period of so-called social development, Bill first showed me the importance of making fun of some traditional things — in a nice way, certainly not in a malicious way. As an example, at one class Bill and his buddies brought BB's and rolled them on the dance floor. This very strict, formal affair certainly changed while four boys gathered up little round balls. I learned about Bill's mischievous side at an early date.

During WWII I was in college in Baltimore and Bill was stationed in the Navy in Washington, DC. His family was living in Washington while his father worked for the War Production Board. They invited me to visit one weekend. Before this period in her life, Bill's mother never had to cook. She was trying to give me a lovely breakfast and decided to make waffles. As waffles will do — they were sticking. Bill took over and demonstrated his ability to solve problems and we had pancakes before we knew it. Bill taught me early in our relationship that there is a *solution* to every problem.

We got married on June 27, 1947, and after our honeymoon returned to Lafayette, Indiana, for Bill to continue his college education at Purdue University. He had solved our housing problem for the summer by talking Dr. Knight, the head of the Psychology Department, into loaning us his home until the fall semester began. Dr. Knight said he would be gone when we arrived, but there the dear man sat when we drove up. He then told us he'd be leaving in the morning. I thought I should be polite so I asked what I could fix him for breakfast (I had something like cereal in mind). He replied, "Finnan Haddie." Shortly I left the room to go upstairs and cry. I couldn't cook at all, and certainly not Finnan Haddie. Problem solver Bill appeared carrying my only cook book which he had given me in hopes that he would not starve. He found the recipe for this unknown dish. Now the problem was where to find the ingredients. "Easy," says Bill. "We'll ask Dr. Knight." Surprise! We learned that the Finnan Haddie, all prepared, resided in the freezer. Do you think the psychologist was testing me?

Our next problem was the rose garden that Bill assured the Knights we would care for. He envisioned watering, picking and enjoying these beautiful flowers. What to do when hundreds of bugs came feasting upon them? "Simple," Bill says. One of our bridesmaids, Jane Alexander's family lived in Lafayette. He picked up the phone and told them our dilemma. In less than an hour, Mr. and Mrs. Alexander arrived with spray and pruning shears in hand. They went to work spraying, trimming and teaching us as they went. They also recommended we get a book on gardening. That copy of "Better Homes and Gardens, Garden Know How" stayed with us, tattered and torn, until we moved to La Vida Llena. Another problem was solved, thanks to Bill.

Through the years I have learned that problem solving with Bill often included reading a book. When we brought our first baby, Nancy, home from the hospital we were well equipped with the bassinette, the bath tub with changing table and the works. But we had no knowledge of how to give a bath. Out comes "Dr. Spock." Step by step Bill read me how to properly bathe our daughter. No problem!

In the early days of marriage and motherhood I would express frustration about things being so routine, lacking in creativeness. Bill took ordinary activities and turned them into creative events. If I was cooking some plain pasta, he'd suggest "throwing something else in the pot — be creative." He left what to add up to me. For 60-plus years I have been adding things to the pots; becoming a creative cook. I often made up my own recipes.

Perhaps the most important thing Bill has done for me is tell me, "Do your own thing." During a time when many women were dominated by their husbands and just fulfilling their roles as wives and mothers, I was encouraged to be a leader in the community and make a role for myself. This started right after we moved to Poughkeepsie, New York, where Bill took a job with IBM. We were called upon by the Welcome Wagon Lady. She asked me to help her start a Newcomers' Club. This would mean some time away from home and our baby daughter. Bill's reaction was, "Go do it." For the first meeting of this organization, she had asked Eleanor Roosevelt to speak. (Mrs. Roosevelt happened to be her godmother.) She asked me to introduce her. I said to Bill, "I can't do that. She's one of the world's most famous and important women." Bill's answer to me, "Yes, you can. Go do it." And I did.

Since then I have belonged to a number of groups in various

communities and been honored to be the president or chairman of many. Over the years, Bill's encouragement and confidence in my abilities have made a great difference. The latest, but probably not the last, was pushing me to talk to other women here at La Vida Llena about organizing a women's group similar to the Men's Breakfast group which he headed. This led to talking to Shirley Patterson and Susan Cho about leading such a group. Thus, the Gathering of Women was born. Who knows what influence he'll have on me next? I'd say it has been significant over the years with a lot of love, patience and caring thrown in.

The Sky Was My Way
by
Ann Olander

I was a Depression Era child, born and raised on an isolated farm south of Chicago. Like all other children on farms, regardless of the weather conditions, we walked to a one-room school house over a mile away. Another school included two lower grades. Later we were bussed to the district high school where the total enrollment was about 200 students.

Mother decided early on that careers were important. Due to financial circumstances, she selected nursing for us. Upon high school graduation, my sister and I attended nursing school in Chicago. One of my mother's cousins kept tabs on us. I was only 17 and fell in love with the city. We worked hard. We wore heavily starched uniforms and performed many nursing duties right from the start. With no air conditioning and under strict old-fashioned discipline, we worked long hours. During our breaks from work, we attended classes. We had one day a week off. On that day we usually went either to the 25 cent movie or to an occasional dance where a big band played. We had to have some recreation!

Upon graduation my sister and I worked for a year doing hospital floor duty. I was quickly elevated to a nursery supervisor. But I had a great desire for change and soon went into private duty. I was caring for a middle-aged man when I read in the newspaper that American Airlines was interviewing young, single RNs to attend stewardess school in New York. Without telling anyone, I went to a large downtown Chicago hotel where many young women from various states were being interviewed. To my surprise, I stuck out the grueling process.

Some three weeks later, I was invited to go to the LaGuardia Airport for further interviews. While getting the needed recommendations I received an airline ticket in the mail. I then had to tell my parents and friends what I was up to. They were shocked and surprised that I had done all this without telling anyone. I was surprised too! It was only years later then I realized this one secret action had changed my life forever.

I continued my quest and, happily for me, my parents went to the airport to see me off. I was scared, worried and wondered what in the world I was doing, but I kept on. Twenty-four other young women had also arrived for classes that lasted six weeks. We had thorough physicals, received intensive training regarding our duties, got acquainted with the planes, were taught how to focus on our appearance, and learned to deal effectively with the passengers. I was about to change from my nurse's white starched uniform to an attractive airline stewardess' uniform. We wore light beige uniforms for summer and navy blue ones for winter. We received lots of attention from everyone: our classes were held in a hangar at the airport and we were very visible. Young women in uniforms were hard to ignore. We were all between 5'2" and 5'6" tall, weighed no more than 125 pounds, and none of us wore glasses. We were all registered nurses who were trained to provide comfort and security to the passengers. After much study, I received my certificate and wings, and was hired.

My first base city was Chicago. From there I flew to many large cities where we stayed overnight, enjoyed the many tourist sights and the different personalities of each city. At that time there were no passenger security checks. Stairs were pushed up to the cabin doors and the passengers were personally greeted by the stewardess. There was no cover from inclement weather. Smoking was permitted on board when the seat belt light was off. The only ones with oxygen were the pilots in the cockpit. The passengers were all well-dressed and were served delicious meals. They were also offered current newspapers, magazines, stationery, and chewing gum to relieve air pressure on the ears when landing.

The only anxious flight I ever had was when the landing gear failed on our Douglas DC-3 propeller plane. For safety reasons, we had to circle until sufficient fuel had been used. Finally we landed on the grass on the side of the runway. Luckily, none of the crew or the 21 passengers was hurt.

One morning I was called to arrive early for my flight. I was met by a professional photographer who took many pictures of me, inside and outside the plane. Sometime later my father called to tell me that a "smiling me" was on the side of a Kroger cereal box!

On December 7, 1941, I was called to the cockpit where the Captain informed me that the Japanese had attacked Pearl Harbor. The war brought many changes to our country. It was the end of only nurses being hired as stewardesses. Now college graduates were hired. Our cities for the first time were in brown out (few or no lights at night). The new passengers became military, government officials, business men, and, on my plane, a few luminaries, such as Eleanor Roosevelt, Bob Hope, Jerry Colona and Kate Smith. All passengers were on a priority basis for obtaining seats.

On a flight to Fort Worth, Texas, I had my first experience with racial discrimination. A young black Army private boarded my flight in St. Louis, Missouri. All seven single seats were occupied. He selected a double seat and was immediately confronted by a white male passenger claiming that he could not sit next to him. A gentleman sitting in a single seat rose and offered the Army private his seat. On arrival at the terminal this Army private was directed to the kitchen to eat. During these years, I developed a very deep admiration for all our military.

At about this time on one of my days off, I met the love of my life. He was an intern at a research hospital and was an acquaintance of my apartment mates. We dated when he had time off and the money for transportation. After he received his M.D., he joined the Navy and was assigned to California. Many months later, I was met by a friend who wanted me to guess who was in my apartment. I soon learned that it was Lt. George Olander. The first thing he did was to escort me down the elevator to introduce me to his new 1941 Chevrolet. After getting into the car he asked me to marry him within the next ten days. It was a very short time to make all the necessary preparations. But I resigned my position with the airline, arranged our wedding and soon I was Mrs. George Olander. He became a flight surgeon and was assigned to a Marine fighter squadron. We had a precious year together before he left for the South Pacific.

I returned to my job as a stewardess since the airlines would now employ married women to be stewardesses. My base was in Texas and I flew to Los Angeles and east to Nashville, Tennessee, until my husband returned. He resigned from the Navy and immediately began his surgical residency. In the ensuing years he became a very successful surgeon and I became "Mom" to six wonderful children.

Some of the things I miss in today's air travel are the wonderful things one experiences when flying at lower altitudes and at slower air speeds. It is under these conditions that you can see all the different landscapes and farm lands. There is the feeling of almost reaching out to touch the white fluffy clouds and the sparkling night city lights below. I must also mention that there appears to be a lack of courtesy in both the personnel and the passengers. This seems to be caused by a lack of time and patience in the modern age of speed.

Looking back over these 70 years, I am amazed at the tremendous advancement of air travel. It is indeed a new world in the sky.

I am thankful that I had "the sky" to show me "my way." I appreciate my parents, family, and the many friends who helped me along the way.

Miss 20

by
Shirley L. Patterson

In the fall of 1962, at age 29, I was admitted to the Master's program in Social Work at the University of Kansas for a second master's degree. It was an exciting change for me. For six years, I had worked for the Presbyterian Church in the impoverished inner city of Topeka, Kansas, assisting in the development of social programs (e.g., a neighborhood day care center, a community civic association, youth work camps for home improvement, mobilizing organizations and city council members to provide public housing for people displaced by Urban Renewal). While it had been an extraordinarily fulfilling part of my life working with motivated community people and church staff, I had the feeling that something was missing.

Although I had a seminary education, I was not allowed to vote at regional presbytery meetings and, because of my gender, I was viewed as "secretary" material at local meetings. By the time the '60s rolled around I was ready to be treated as a professional.

While waiting for my first class to begin, I reviewed what I knew about my professor, Esther Elizabeth Twente (yes, 20). In 1933, Miss Twente was recruited by the Sociology Department to teach social work courses with the eventual goal of establishing undergraduate and graduate programs in Social Work. By the spring of 1947, this goal was accomplished and the Department of Social Work was accredited and going strong.[1] When a class bell ring broke through my ruminations about Professor Twente, an interesting looking woman in her mid-sixties strolled into the classroom. She was burdened down with two messy looking briefcases in her hands and she had tennis shoes on her feet. I thought, "Oh, my! I hope I can learn from her." But, when she spoke, I knew I had found my mentor, my role model and, eventually, my colleague and friend.

There is no doubt I could write "volumes" about my nearly decade-long relationship with this remarkable woman whom I always called "Miss Twente" (a mark of respect during that era). However, I will try and let you taste the "flavor" of our relationship over the nine years I knew her prior to her death. As her student, I took every class I could from her. Although my first year field experience was a psychiatric one, my second year practicum was with Esther Twente. She was one of seven persons across the United States who was awarded a three-year Ford Foundation research project. She was awarded the project on Aging in Marion County, Kansas.

During the summer and three days a week for the following year, I slept on an Army cot in Miss Twente's rented apartment kitchen located over a liquor store in Hillsboro, Kansas. My mind was almost stretched to the brink by our Socratic evening conversations and daytime experiences with older people exploring their "potentials and capacities" for creativity. People's strengths (i.e., potentials and capacities) always were Esther Twente's focus in relating to people personally, academically, and professionally. This Ford Foundation Project resulted in a book, *Never Too Old.*[2] The

---

1 Shirley Patterson and Ben Zimmerman, eds., *Transitions: The Emergence, Growth, and Development of the School of Social Welfare* (Lawrence, Kansas: University of Kansas Printing Service, 1987).
2 Esther E. Twente, *Never Too Old: The Aged in Community Life* (San Francisco: Jossey-Bass Inc., Publishers, 1970).

thesis of this book was the earliest effort to document the abilities of older people to lead interesting and productive lives. This viewpoint recognized potentials and capacities at a time when the world did not view older people in quite that way. This has become known as the Strengths Model in social work practice.

Throughout the remaining seven years of our relationship, Miss Twente helped me "own" this concept in every endeavor I undertook. She served as an unpaid consultant to me when I became Director of Crosslines Family Counseling Center in the Kansas City, Kansas, Poverty Program helping me identify the potentials and capacities of my three indigenous family aides (one of whom was a high school dropout who eventually got her G.E.D. and went on to receive a master's degree in Social Work). Miss Twente also continued to encourage me to reach my full potential by supporting my efforts to write and receive a three year project on "natural helping" from the National Institutes of Mental Health. She urged me to apply for and graduate from the Ph.D. Program in Social Work at the University of Wisconsin-Madison. Perhaps the dearest thing I learned from her was how to repair the fan belt of my VW Bug. One day on the way to a meeting in Marion County the fan belt broke. Miss Twente took out two large safety pins and calmly reattached the broken ends. We continued on our mission.

What I remember most about that first class with Miss Twente was a story about her chaplain friend at the VA Hospital in Topeka who had been born without arms or legs. By the time he reached manhood, completed his education and started to work, he could type by holding a pencil in his mouth and tapping on the keys with the eraser end, maneuver a wheel chair with the stubs of his arms, and drive a car through the miracle of modern automotive science. The Chaplain's oft repeated maxim was "always 'greet' what remains of a person: never what is lost." This simple, but complex, idea has guided both my personal and professional life. I recall, when I was teaching second year graduate students, a young woman quadriplegic came up to me after class and said how much she appreciated me because I was the only professor she had who was not embarrassed to look her directly in the eye when speaking to her. Yes, always greet what remains of a person.

In my 35 years of university teaching and relating to people I know and cherish, Miss Twente's holistic views, coupled with my own, have guided my life. Or, to put it in a more edible way, this was "the frosting on my cake!" In 1971 Miss Twente died of a metastasized cancer at age 76. The day before she died, I held her hand while she was in a coma and told her I loved her.

Operation Homecoming – An Extraordinary Lesson
by
Regina Resley

The large United States Air Force airplane came gently gliding down to the runway at Clark Air Force Base on Luzon Island in the Philippines. It was February 14, 1973, about four o'clock on a hot muggy afternoon. This event and its aftermath have stayed with me for years. That airplane carried the first one hundred prisoners of war (POW's) from Hanoi, North Vietnam, to freedom. Some of those men had been in captivity by the North Vietnamese for eight years. The Cease Fire had gone into affect in early January. Negotiations continued for the next two months. The U.S. military forces were being sent home from South Vietnam and more POW's would be returned in increments until the end of March.

The day that plane landed I had just finished volunteering with a Girl Scout troop of Brownies. My 15-year-old daughter, who had been helping me, stood holding my hand as we waited for the buses to bring the POW's past us on the way to the Base Hospital. This was exciting and the anticipation was almost overwhelming. The notice had gone out to everyone on the Base to not go to the flight line. The officials had no idea what the responses or the conditions of the POW's would be like. Despite this order the streets were lined with servicemen, families, and civilians cheering and clapping with tears flowing freely from all of us. Our son, a senior in high school, had gone to the flight line with friends and saw the ceremony as the POW's came down those steps to freedom.

The POW's were hanging out the windows of the buses, crying and yelling, "Thank you," with huge grins and smiles on their faces. One POW was waving a small U.S. flag he had made and hidden somewhere on him. The crowds were clapping and calling, "Thank you. We love you. Welcome home." The POW's were wearing the black pajama-style clothes they had worn as prisoners. They looked so wan and tired. They were thin and you could see exhaustion in their expressions. The weeping and joy was all there from the POW's and everyone along the way. Those dumpy old green Army school buses were actually carrying heroes, kings and emperors past their subjects.

My husband was an Army officer and had been assigned as the Army Advisor at Tinh Bien Tuy, a province in South Vietnam. Our family lived with him on Clark Air Base while he was on this assignment.

I volunteered for the Red Cross at overseas postings. At this post my first volunteer job was at the Base Hospital. In December, 12 volunteers were asked by the Red Cross Director to be part of the team who would work with POW's when they entered the hospital. Our assignment was to be quiet. We were to tell no one, including family, what we would be doing. The officials were concerned that information would be leaked early to news reporters or others.

When the officials decided the first stop on the way home for the POW's would be Clark Air Base Hospital, decisions had to be made. One of them was that the hospital would be closed to all but emergencies. Another was the POW's would stay for three days so some health tests could be run. There would be an Escort for each one. The Escorts were to have extensive discussions with the

POW's informing them of changes in family matters and events that would affect their new lives. The information given to them needed to include deaths, divorces, and remarriages: all of the things to bring them up to date on happenings during their imprisonment.

After these discussions, the volunteers scheduled the POW's first phone calls to their families. When the first group had made their calls, it was discovered that news reporters had obtained permission to be present at the first phone calls. The Escorts then had to be sure to tell the POW's that their first remarks might be heard around the world.

Schools on the Base and around the United States sent posters and letters of welcome to the POW's. We would tape these on the walls leading to the cafeteria and the POW's would sign or write notes on them. After the POW's left for the States, we would send the letters and posters back to the originating schools. Sometimes we would take the prison pajamas-style clothes home to wash because the POW's wanted to take them home. We baked cookies for the Day Room and found ourselves pressing shirts or uniforms.

The courage of these men was an inspiration to everyone. They arrived at the hospital with their spirits bruised and pounded. They were thrilled and amazed that their ordeal was over and they were free. But they also knew how much was missing from their lives that could never return.

One of the very first things that happened was they were given new uniforms to wear the next day. The change was dramatic. When they entered the hospital they were tired and dragging. Wearing those uniforms the next day, they were upright, smiling and joking. Life was worth living. The transformation was unbelievable. They were military again and proud of all they went through. You could see it in their bearing. I learned from them that having control of your spirit, faith and courage can carry you through whatever is out there waiting for you.

The next two planes of returnees found the entire Base personnel lining the road cheering, crying and waving. These men had given all they could for us and we wanted them to know we realized what the cost was for them. The admiration and respect for those brave men was a lesson for all of us.

Operation Homecoming will always have a special place in our family. Some Americans at that time marched against the Vietnam War which was their right. But never again should we vilify the fighting man who is doing his duty to our country. It was a privilege to be around those POW's to see and learn first hand what bravery and courage is. How they could survive their experience and still love and respect humanity is a powerful lesson.

How did this experience change me? It turned me into an ongoing optimist. On our return from overseas, I was asked to become an Arlington Lady. These women attend military funerals at Arlington National Cemetery. This was a once a month, five year commitment. Some days we attended four funerals. During each funeral we would give a note to the widow thanking her for the service of her husband. Each of these encounters was emotional and hard to do. When it was difficult I would think of those Vietnam POW's and the duty they performed.

My attitude about life is that you do your best and encourage those around you. All the events in life are challenges and can be faced and conquered with an optimistic attitude. Let's just say I don't worry about small everyday things. I learned from those POW's that life is a gift and precious to each of us. It can never be taken for granted. Life can change in an instant and you need to keep your spirits up by realizing that you, alone, can control your attitude. When you feel comfortable with yourself and try to understand the feelings of others, you can face and solve any adversity. The courage to live is inside me. I learned that from those POW's who survived such horror, came home to families and friends, picked up their lives and moved on. Several of them became Senators and Representatives. They went back to their communities and continued with their lives. What I learned from those brave men taught me that I can change my life in any way; it is just up to me and my attitude.

Mother's Love
by
Mary Ansel Roney

As I look back over my life, I have very few regrets. I might have married a rancher in Nebraska; I could have become an airline stewardess; or a teaching position could have sounded more interesting some place other than New Mexico. But as my choices and the results developed, I have been happy, content and am convinced my parents and the love and support they afforded me from birth until their  death is responsible for my feeling of self-worth and happiness.

My mother was more involved with the lives of my brother and me. My father became ill when we were very young. He was loving and able to continue his work as a rural mail carrier, but Mother made most of the family decisions.

Mother came to Oklahoma from Nebraska with her family in a covered wagon. Her mother was ill and the doctor had told my grandfather that a lower and drier climate might improve her health. They established a homestead near Elk City, Oklahoma. There she was able to attend the one-room Red Rock School sporadically when her mother was well enough to be left alone. She always regretted not having a better education and was determined that we stay in school. After her death, we found a number of books on various subjects she had studied.

During the Great Depression we were more fortunate than many, because my father was working. Our house was on a corner and the back door was easily reached from the street. Mother's back door was well known by those who were hungry. They were always greeted kindly and given something to eat. Even as a small child, I remember the compassion she had for those who were in need of help.

One day a family came to our front door selling willow furniture they had made. As they were talking, I was watching and listening. They said they needed money to buy food. Mother was very complimentary about their furniture and said she felt badly about their situation, but she couldn't afford to buy any furniture. She returned to her work in the house. About an hour later a neighbor, who lived on the next street, called to tell her that I was at her house with the people selling furniture. I had taken it upon myself to go and help these people. I would knock on doors and encourage the neighbors to buy the furniture. No one ever told me whether or not I was any help when it came to selling — but I sure wanted to help like I saw Mother doing.

Mother was active in the Christian Church. That church community matched Mother's commitment to providing a loving place for children and her concern for others. I could never remember a time when I did not go to Sunday school and church weekly. By the time I was 4 or 5 years old, I was completely comfortable reciting poetry or scripture in front of a group of people.

We lived in a town, as did many of my friends at school; but some of the girls I knew lived in the country. Years later, several of these friends told me how much they enjoyed coming to our house, because mother was so friendly and they always felt welcome.

I never remember getting a spanking. Mother would talk sternly to me as punishment. She was always there for my brother and

158

me. I can't remember wanting to do anything bad. Once when I was in high school, a boy from another town had come to visit and we drove around town in his car. When I came home, Mother smelled smoke on my clothes because he had been smoking in the car. She thought I had been smoking and I was crushed that she could even think I would do such a thing. I wanted to be good because she expected me to be good.

When my husband and I had our first child and I held him for the first time, I was overwhelmed with the love I felt. It was then I knew how much my mother and father had loved me. Just as my brother and I always came first with Mother, his children came first with him and my children come first with me.

I taught school before I was married and went back to doing substitute teaching when my children started to school. It broke my heart when I knew the children I taught didn't have support at home. My husband died when my children were in high school. When they were in college, I went back for a master's degree. I taught remedial reading and had small classes. It gave me the opportunity for one-on-one teaching and I could let my students know that I really cared. I felt that was the best thing I could do for them: let them know that it mattered to me that they could read. It was much like it mattered to my mother that I did well. She didn't expect me to make straight A's, but to do the best I could.

Mother passed on her love to my children, as well. She enjoyed having them come to visit in the summer and usually had a project they could help with. One year, when my son was about 12 years old, he had been working on an electricity project in 4-H. When he arrived at my mother's, he replaced all the switches in her house. This gave him a great feeling of satisfaction.

Usually Mother would involve my daughter in some redecorating undertaking. My daughter would help Mother sew curtains, paint, paper, refinish furniture, etc. Several years later, my daughter received her B.A. degree in Interior Design and now has her own business in that field.

When Mother died, she was buried in Elk City, Oklahoma. Her home there was still intact. All her children and grandchildren were present for her funeral and for decisions about how to disperse her belongings. She had put names on many things that individuals had told her they liked, so that item could be given to that person. But there were many things in the house that were not spoken for. Now this situation can sometimes bring about rancor and jealousy in families. But not ours. We arranged ourselves by age, oldest first (that was me). Then, one at a time, we went through the house to pick one thing we wanted. When the last person had chosen something, we started at the beginning of the row again until everything was spoken for.

There was no bickering among the family. Everyone agreed this was the fair way to do it and each respected the other's choice. It was the loving way Mother would have wanted us to distribute her belongings. All of her furniture and accessories are now present in a family member's home; just as her love is present in each of us and passed on to those we love.

Instructor of Piano – Instructor of Life
by
Betty Jo Sargent

Mrs. Donna Stuart taught me music and through music she taught me discipline, persistence, patience and proficiency in a skill. Through it all I developed self-confidence to carry me through the rest of my life.

My childhood was spent in a small inland town beside a beautiful lake. Entertainment was mostly through activities on the lake, concerts by the high school band, baseball, football, cowboys and rodeos. Cultural events such as the Community Concert series were held in the next largest town. To attend meant driving 40 miles at night.

One day Mrs. Donna Stuart and her husband came to town with two pianos. They brought music and lots more to our town and to me. Mrs. Stuart soon had a busy schedule of piano students. She was my piano teacher from fifth grade through high school. Students from beginner to advanced were given quality music. Recitals were held several times a year. Our music pieces always had to be memorized. At these programs I envied the older students who could play big impressive chords. But, I needed patience to grow. Mrs. Stuart wisely selected classical compositions appropriate for small hands. Playing at a recital developed my ability to carry on in spite of distractions, such as a ringing telephone or a fire truck passing by.

I was a busy kid during my school years. There was summer camp, Camp Fire Girls, a three-member "Red Bicycle Detective Club," and swimming in the lake with my dog. Mrs. Stuart realized that I needed discipline to practice. Together we worked out a schedule for after-school time. The structure gave time for school assignments, practice and recreation.

When I was in high school, I was playing compositions by Mozart, Beethoven, Chopin and others. Mrs. Stuart approached the idea of my giving a senior recital. "What ME?" I was dumbfounded, but got right to work. For the finale, I began learning the Mendelssohn Piano Concerto in G minor (20 pages to memorize). A fellow student and friend played the orchestral arrangement on a second piano. The recital was a formal affair with long dresses, printed programs, flowers and an article in the local newspaper. I now appreciate the time, work and expense Mrs. Stuart put into that program.

I was a shy student in high school and never spoke up in class, but I could memorize. Music gave me a skill — an area where I could shine. And, most of all, music gave me a way to gain self-confidence.

The next big decision in my life was choosing a college to attend. I needed Mrs. Stuart to help. She wanted me to find a school where I would not be a little frog in an enormous puddle. I was admitted to a small, respected liberal arts college as a music major.

The time I had as a student with Mrs. Stuart I now see as a very important time. She gave me a lifetime of skills: discipline, patience and proficiency in music. She helped me develop the self-confidence to make more of the rest of my life. For all these I am grateful.

Not a Place
by
Mary Ellen Simms

In my sixth year, the summer days were long and filled with sunshine, fresh air and adventures. Located on several acres, the compound where my family lived was an almost magical place. A hospital, where my father was the sole physician, was located on a private road across the street from our home. There was a wide expanse of lawn between our home and that of the engineer who kept the hospital, homes and grounds working smoothly.

To the left were several small connected apartments occupied by the nursing staff. Stretched over the grounds were dozens of trees covered with vines where one could swing over the many ditches to imitate Tarzan and Jane. Across another road an acre of trees provided a perfect place to play hide-and-seek. Safe and secure, my father, mother, brother and I were the "Happy Family."

From December 7, 1941, on there was a shift in the air that even a 6, almost 7, year-old could sense. Without understanding what or why, I knew something was different. Small changes began to appear — even though our father continued to cross the road to the hospital each day, our mother kept our home comfortable and happy, and

John and I walked to school each day. New family friends were visiting our home and an unfamiliar name, Camp Gruber, began to creep into conversations. We were remotely aware our country was at war, but it all became real when we were told our father had enlisted in the Army. Camp Gruber was no longer a mysterious name, but an Army training post, just 40 miles away, that was to become our father's residence. Mother, John and I moved to an apartment close to the town we had always known. Our father was home many weekends and we were still safe and secure and the "Happy Family."

I became accustomed to our new residence and the comings and goings of my father, but slowly became aware that more changes were on the way. The newspapers and the movie news reels brought the war closer to home and our parents did not keep reality from us. I understood my father could be sent overseas and that I might not see him again, but the idea seemed far away. We would remain in our apartment in the town we loved until he came home and our lives became as they once were: safe and secure in our compound surrounded by trees and vines with Tarzan and Jane and hide-and-seek again a big part of life.

Plans were being made and boxes were being packed before I finally realized that not only was change on the way — it had arrived. It was not to be believed, but our father was leaving the United States. We would be leaving the town we loved and would live up north in Wisconsin with our father's mother, our Nana. Not only would we be in a new town, house and school, but our mother would be leaving us and working many miles away as a nurse. I was not aware of how homesick I would become or how much the next year and a half would change me.

In short order, I learned about the changes in weather. Having spent most of my life in Oklahoma, I was not accustomed to short summers and long winters. Swimming in a cold lake was quite different than the warm river I had known. Snowsuits and boots were fun at the beginning, but grew tiresome as winter never seemed to end. Sledding and ice skating were brand new and fun to learn. Although, I didn't excel in either. What I remember most was the first flower peeking through the snow and realizing spring was on its way. Flowers have never been more beautiful than they were that day.

Walking to school was not a new experience and school rooms were the same everywhere. However, being the only new student in my fifth grade class was a big change. I had many lessons to learn and some would prove to be quite painful. The teacher, Miss Brown, chastised me for saying, "Yes, Ma'am." She did not seem to know that was a sign of respect.

The other students made fun of my Oklahoma twang and my messy hair. When report card time came, Miss Brown told me my parents would be very disappointed with my grades. I don't remember the grades, but I do remember thinking, "How do you know? You don't know my parents." I did become a part of the class and the other children accepted me, although my best friends were found in books I loved. Throughout my life the love of books has remained a part of me.

Nana's house became home. The room prepared for me was upstairs and I was excited by the wall paper and the bay window with a window seat. John slept in the room next to mine and Nana was across the landing. The downstairs bedroom was for guests and for Mother on her visits. There was a coal burning stove in the kitchen where we ran to dress on those cold winter mornings. I did not realize how hard Nana worked to keep the coal furnace working or how difficult it must have been to provide the good meals we ate. These changes in my home life seemed to come easily and I accepted them.

What did not come easily was the absence of both parents. I was consumed with homesickness for our town and the life we had there. We could not return to that life and our father could not come to us, but our mother could and did. In time things became easier for all of us and we were grateful.

These were years when I learned many things. Nana taught me how to hang the wash on the clothes line, the proper way to wash dishes and how to pull weeds in the garden. I earned my first salary in the canning factory's green bean field. I still remember how good the cold, hard 50-cent piece felt in my hand. I was puzzled to hear people talk about the terrible way the "colored" were treated in the South when the treatment of American Indian tribes in Wisconsin was so bad. I became aware that the country where I lived was bigger than just the place where I lived and that others loved their towns as much as I loved mine. There was ice in my bedroom water bowl on winter mornings and heated bricks wrapped in flannel to warm my bed at night. My brother could be a very good friend, as well as someone to fight with. Though sugar and butter were rationed, Nana found a way to bake cookies for after-school treats.

The war ended, and my father came home. We returned to the compound in the town I loved. It didn't last, of course, and it was never the same. Our family moved on and, although I still missed that town I loved, I found that it was my father, mother, brother and I that made a "Happy Family" — not a place.

"Me, a Woman, Running for City Council?"
by
Connie Thompson

My late husband, James C. Thompson, an attorney, had a great influence in my life.

One day at breakfast in 1978, while reading the newspaper, I said something about not liking what was going on at the Española City Hall. He said to me, "Why don't you do something about it and run for a seat on the City Council." I responded, "Me, a woman, running for the City Council? The Council is all men, including the Mayor. Nine men altogether." My brother came in at that time and also urged me to run for a Council seat. After two or three days of thinking about it, I decided to go for it.

I started campaigning door to door and was quite encouraged. However, at one family home, the head of the family, a man with about 18 votes, said he could not vote for me because I was a woman. At that time, the head of the family "directed" the other family members how to vote. I mentioned this to my father that evening and my father said he would go see him. When my father returned, he said Mr. Vigil and his family would vote for me. I asked him what changed the man's mind, and my father responded, "I told him, 'My daughter, as a woman, has more guts to serve on the City Council than all the men on it.'"

I continued campaigning. However, on the Thursday before the election the following Tuesday, I went skiing and broke my leg. On Election Day, my husband took me to the polling place, set up a card table with my campaign literature and brought a chair for me to sit on and another chair on which to place my casted leg. I sat there, visited with the voters and asked for their vote. At the end of the day, after the ballots were counted, I had won by 66 votes over two opponents.

While I was recuperating from my broken leg, my husband went to City Hall and picked up City ordinances, personnel information, etc. which I read and digested while I was laid up with my broken leg. At the swearing in ceremony, my husband held me up. I placed my hand on the Bible, raised my right hand and was sworn in. After that, he drove me to the Council meetings.

As a City Council member, I was successful in obtaining approval and coordinating the building of a new sewage treatment plant, and opening more through-streets. I went out of my way to meet the City employees to determine what each one did at their job. Since I had read the ordinances and other City government materials, I was well versed in the City's operations; more so than the men on the Council.

The City of Española was a member of the New Mexico Municipal League. I became active on behalf of the City and was elected President of the League. The New Mexico Municipal League was a member of the National League of Cities. I attended meetings in Washington, DC, ran for a seat on the 26-member Board of Directors and won a seat on that Board.

The City and I started working on economic development and ideas on how to bring companies to the Española Valley that would provide jobs and revenues to the Española Valley. Some of these companies were providing support services to the Los Alamos National Laboratory. The City bought a tract of land for an industrial park where companies could build and locate their operations.

I reached out to the state of New Mexico's Economic Development Department. The purpose of this department was to encourage companies to locate in New Mexico and provide jobs and revenues. A group of us, from around the country, who were involved in economic development, met at the White House with the inter-governmental group. President Reagan met with us for a short meeting.

When Bruce King was elected Governor of New Mexico, he appointed me to the New Mexico Arts Commission, which is now the Cultural Affairs Commission. I chaired the Arts Commission for four years. The Board was comprised of 12 members. I then became a member of the National Arts Advocacy Group and became a member, and later the Chair, of one of its committees.

After my four year experience on the Española City Council, I made a decision to run for Mayor against two opponents. I won by 60 votes and served as Mayor for four years during which there was considerable growth in the city. In conjunction with the City Council I worked to obtain as many city services as possible — more roads, an expansion of our sewage treatment plant and improved employee benefits.

I used the experience I gained while campaigning for the City Council and Mayor and serving in these capacities, to reach out to members of the City Council and staff. I asked them for their ideas and thoughts on what the city's needs were and how we could generate interest in passing laws on planning and zoning. We also discussed how we could best apply for funding from state and federal agencies to build infrastructure the city needed. I got many ideas from simply listening to people. These activities gave me a wealth of experience which further enriched my life.

That comment by my husband over breakfast pushed me into being active in city government and all the other community and national organizations and boards to which I belonged. I learned a lot from these experiences. By reaching out to the City Council, staff and city residents for advice and ideas, I learned how to interact with people and the best ways to get results. I learned how to evaluate ideas and make choices.

I used these experiences in making personal choices. After four years as Mayor, my husband was diagnosed with Parkinson's disease. Rather than run for re-election as Mayor, I left city politics to care of my husband with the help of my daughters and a professional nurse. When my husband passed away, I moved from Española to Albuquerque to be close to my daughter, Chrissy Akes, and her two children.

When selling my home and property in Española, buying a house in Albuquerque and interacting with realtors and contractors, I was able to utilize skills I honed while in city politics. My experience working with the city budget helped me discuss, evaluate and create a personal budget so I could make the decision to sell my home and move to La Vida Llena, a retirement community. The experience further allowed me to make independent decisions on purchases and travel. I constantly interact with my daughters, friends and relatives and now live a richer life by making the best possible choices.

I am grateful for my husband who influenced me to explore new opportunities that not only have created cherished memories, but supported my abilities, as a woman, to move into politics — traditionally, a man's field.

No Such Thing
by
Mary Ann Wade

There is no time of greater cer-
tainty in your life than when you are
young and sassy: you've sorted out
just how the world is put together;
you know for a fact just what is true in
it and what is not true. It is during that
time of naive smugness that the world
pounces and turns your brain upside
down, for you need to be taught that
what you see is not always what you
are looking at.

In 1971 our young family of five lived in Charlottesville, Virginia, the gracious historic and cultural center of Albemarle County.
The whole area was tastefully dotted with enormous estates built
during a time of carriage houses, vast hay fields and slave labor. My
husband, a forester, had done some timber work for a landowner
who called him up one day and asked if we would be willing to stay
out at his place for a year while he took care of business overseas.
Astonished, we thought about it, and said, "Yes."

Built in 1830 out of bricks formed in the yard from the red clay
of Albemarle County, "Ernscliff" had been a quiet witness to political, structural and familial changes for over a century, all the while
presiding over thousands of acres of pasture and woodlands, plant-

ings and harvests, births and deaths. We thought that house sitting there for a year would be a unique experience, sort of a "how-the-other-half-lives" adventure; so we packed up our three little children, some household stuff and the dog, and moved to Ernscliff. Well, it was unique all right.

One morning in late winter our 2-year-old twins called me upstairs. They had climbed onto a deep window sill in the hall near their room. "Ree," they said, pointing out the window. I looked, and all I saw was the widow's walk that encircled the roof over the kitchen. "Ree, Mommy!"

"Do you mean 'tree'? I can see some treetops out there."

"No Mommy, REE!" And they waved in recognition.

Odd. So what was a "ree"? Ree. Tree. Cloud. Roof. Fence. Bird. No — had to be a tree out there. I shook my head and went on with our day.

That night after the children were in bed I wandered into the living room and lit the fire I had laid in the fireplace that morning. The fireplace was so big and old and deep you could get your thoughts lost in there. Its warmth spread toward me as I curled myself into a wing chair and opened a book. Lamplight gentled the flickering shadows around me, and I was almost at peace. But not quite. This old house was beginning to yield its secrets.

Ree. I put the book down. Who — or what — was Ree? I thought again about the strange evening last week when we were all in that very room reading bedtime stories, and we heard booted footsteps slowly walking across the floor of the spare bedroom above us. But it turned out that no one was up there.

And now Ree.

I stared into the fire and wondered about it. Could it be – no, it couldn't be — but maybe we had a ghost? I blinked and gripped the arms of my chair. OK, get rational, I told myself. There is no way we had a ghost. Ghosts are in cartoons, or horror stories about old haunted houses at Halloween, and who took those seriously? The twins probably saw out there a bird or a squirrel they named "Ree." And maybe last week a critter fell into the chimney of the spare room upstairs and thumped all over the floor trying to find a way out, and we just thought it sounded like footsteps.

But Ernscliff was old, after all. Generations of families had lived there. I knew so little about them. Did the women climb the stairs with their little ones at bedtime and sing sleepy songs to them as I did? I wondered if they had loved the deep windows too, and the high ceilings that kept you cool in the summer, and all the fireplaces. What did they put into the nooks and crannies that now held wisps of dust bunnies from long ago? Did they sit before this very fireplace, contemplating the known and the unknown as I did?

Then a man with dark hair and a clipped beard walked slowly past the living room door. He was of slight stature, and wore an old-fashioned black suit with a vest and a collarless white shirt open at the throat. He looked at me curiously, then continued down the hall.

My heart thumped. Who was *that*? How did he get in? I picked up a heavy candlestick, took a deep breath, and went out into the hall. No one was there. I tiptoed across the hall to the study where my husband was working. "Greg," I said unsteadily, "was someone here with you? I saw a man in the hall and he isn't there now and…"

My husband grabbed a pistol out of his desk drawer and checked the doors. They were locked and bolted, as we had left them. We searched the house, upstairs and down. We looked in every room, behind every door, under every bed, over every cabinet. Twice. Nothing. We guarded the sleeping children, but no sleep came to us that night.

What had just happened? Was somebody in the house after all? Did that man know a secret way out? Why didn't our dog bark? Did I see a ghost? Was it Ree? Had the man lived here before? Had he died here, for God's sake? Was he only curious about who was in his house now, or was he trying to scare us away? I never did feel that he wanted to do us any harm. Are there really such things as ghosts after all? I mean, everybody knows there aren't. But who made those footsteps overhead? And if it was Ree, why could the twins see him from the window and I couldn't? But I *did* see someone in the hall, at least for a moment. Seen or unseen, that little man was *there*. Such thoughts tumbled around the inside of my head all night long.

As morning light eased the deep shadows that surrounded us, our 6-year-old daughter appeared in front of me and wanted to know why we were sitting in the hall with yesterday's clothes on and not our PJ's.

"Well, we thought we'd stay up here near you," I said.

"Why?"

"Something happened last night that surprised us," I said carefully, "and we wanted to make sure you and the twins were going to be all right."

Linda crawled into my lap. "What happened, Mommy?"

I put my arms around her. "OK. This is going to sound weird, but here goes. Do you remember Ree?"

"You mean Ree that Stephen and Jason could see, but I couldn't?"

"Yes, that Ree. You know, I never saw him either. But maybe I did last night."

Her eyes got big. "You saw Ree?"

"Maybe," I said. "But not out the window. Downstairs in the hall outside the living room." And I told her what he looked like, and the scary part that he wasn't there when I stood up and peeked into the hall. "So you see," I said, "maybe it was Ree, but maybe it wasn't. It might have been somebody else."

"Somebody else?" she whispered. "You mean we have *two* ghosts?"

"I don't know, Sweetheart. I just don't know," I said slowly.

She rubbed my arm. "Mommy, were you scared?"

"Oh, yes, I was then, but I'm not now."

"Mommy. You should of woke me up. I could help. And Stephen and Jason know Ree and they could of told him to stop scaring you."

I could feel the sudden sting of tears as I hugged that brave little girl.

We never did hear the footsteps overhead again. The twins didn't wave to Ree anymore. And I never again saw the little man with the curious eyes. Ever. But, throughout my life, I have been open to the possibility of "things" being not quite as they may seem to be. These possibilities continue to enrich my existence.

Joan, My Yorkshire Cousin
by
Constance "Connie" Walker

Aunt Ruth Mann had always maintained communication with our British cousins in and near Skipton in North Yorkshire, England. When I was in college during World War II, she encouraged me to write to our cousin, Ernest Higson, serving in the Royal Air Force. This was something I enjoyed doing, but he married and I married in the post war years and by 1974, the correspondence had ceased.

My husband, Don, and I had raised two children and had begun to think about travelling abroad. At that time, our foreign travel had consisted of a few hours in Mexico and occasional short trips to Ontario, Canada, when we lived in Michigan.

We were living in Maryland with government jobs; his was Federal and mine was with the county's library system, specifically Davis Regional Library in Bethesda. Rose Miller managed this rather large public library. She loved travelling and inspired her staff to use vacation time to expand their travel experiences. She was a goldmine of information and, of course, we had resources on our reference and circulating shelves.

Don and I began planning in January 1974 with regular advice from Rose. I wrote Aunt Ruth for an update on Ernest's address because we chose England for our initial journey across the sea. Naturally, I would want to meet my British family when I had the opportunity. And this is where Joan enters the story. Ernest had married Joyce, but he had two married sisters: the older one, Dorothy Bateson and the younger, Joan Southwell. Our AAA travel agent outlined a loop tour for us which would place us, for four days, in a hotel in Ilkley, Yorkshire, just down the road from Skipton. On May 17, 1974, we would meet.

What a wonderful warm family friendship it has been these 37 years! On that first visit there were four of us American tourists: our daughter, Margaret, on vacation from Indiana University; her friend, Christine; Don and me. In our rented car, we located the Higson house on the main road through Skipton. That evening we were taken to an attractive country inn for dinner with their extended family. The group might have been a dozen or more.

We were occupied the next day with local sightseeing at Skipton Castle and in the surrounding countryside, much of which is in the Yorkshire Dales National Park. Ernest was a perfect guide then and on later trips.

Dinner time came again and this evening was our opportunity to go to Green Bank Farm, the home of Joan and Andy Southwell. There was even more of my British family there. Joyce and Joan were the stars of the evening with their spectacular cooking including the marvelous dessert, Trifle. We had driven west of Skipton on a country road going through pastures surrounded by stone walls. This is sheep-raising country and Andy was responsible for lots of them.

The next two days exposed us to pretty villages and the ruins of Bolton Abbey in a wide green valley, called Wharfedale. This is also the land of James Herriot, the famous and beloved veterinarian, and on a subsequent trip Ernest treated us to his "James Herriot tour". But this time the four of us Americans were scheduled to continue on to such places as the coast of Wales and Winston

Churchill's birthplace, Blenheim Palace. We had to move on.

Don and I returned to Britain in 1976 and again in 1979. Both times we were delighted to visit in the homes of Ernest and Joyce and Joan and Andy. It is obvious we had become Anglophiles.

We retired in 1983 and moved from the National Capital area to North Carolina, but traveling was still on the agenda. Andy died in 1984 and Joan had left the farm to live in a smaller house in the town of Embsay, within walking distance of Skipton. Our trips to England in 1986 and 1988 did not offer us the pleasure of Andy's company. In 1990 Joyce, a victim of cancer, had also passed away. But, always there were the welcome letters regularly arriving from Ernest and Joan, brother and sister.

Skipton was a starting point for travelers with a tour company, named Wallace Arnold. It was one with which Ernest and Joan and their spouses had become acquainted. In 1992, reservations were made with Wallace Arnold for a trip to Austria with "double occupancy" rooms belonging to Don and Ernest or Joan and Connie in each hotel. We were eager to expand our list of countries visited. Joan loves to travel and Ernest was studying German at the time.

Joan and I would become compatible roommates with each other and companion-travelers with the two men, in both Europe and the United States. She loved tea breaks and always travelled with accompanying "sweets." On that first trip by our foursome, we were enriched by scenes of a different kind than British, although we departed on a comfortable coach from and returned on it to Skipton. Several days were spent in a Tyrolean town, named Nassereith, which offered charming walking paths and delicious new menus. The tour included a short cruise on the Rhine River, a look into the Heidelberg cafe that inspired "The Student Prince," and a tour through the fairytale castle, "Neuschwanstein," built by King Ludwig. Crossing the Chanel on the ferry between Calais and Dover — the return trip — was a rough and lengthy experience I will never forget.

179

The following May and June we were able to return Ernest and Joan's hospitality. They flew to Greenville, South Carolina, where we met them and provided some relaxation in our North Carolina house. This was followed by a tour of the Eastern States in our station wagon. This, too, was an opportunity for the U.S. family to enjoy time with the Englanders. We joined our daughter and grandson in Virginia, continued into Washington, DC, and made stops at The White House and the museums on the National Mall. Next was New England. Aunt Ruth had died — the years were claiming loved ones. Ruth's daughter acted as a hostess to their foreign cousins, while Don and I drove to New Brunswick for a few days. We all returned to the Carolinas and finally, before their farewell, visited the Low Country and Charleston for a look at the beautiful plantations.

Joan remained a widowed single woman and trustworthy professional secretary with the same Skipton company during the 1990s. She and I remained in close communication, regularly reporting to each other about our activities and our families. Losses of loved ones occurred in my life, too. In 1994, I lost my mother to cancer and our daughter, Margaret, in an auto accident.

Don and I had made the important decision to enjoy the second part of our retirement in a retirement community, La Vida Llena, in Albuquerque, New Mexico. His sudden death, from a heart attack, occurred within days of our completed move from North Carolina. Family and friends were extremely caring and kind; I knew Don had been totally in favor of the move we had just successfully completed — as I had been. October 2, 1995, was the first day of the rest of my life.

A favorite American cousin from Tijeras, New Mexico, became my new best friend and was of immense help as I began to settle down in my new location. Eventually, I made travel plans and found journeys back to Europe and to all parts of the United States enriching my life. In 2000, with my sister and her husband, I returned to England. We were part of a Grand Circle Travel tour of

Britain whose itinerary included a two-day stop in York. What a pleasure it was to meet Ernest and Joan again, if only for lunch and a chat in our hotel.

Old age caught up with Ernest. Since our happy reunion in York, he has been living comfortably in an assisted living facility. However, Joan and I continued to stay in touch and travel together.

First, came a 2003 Sun Tour bus trip which included National Parks in Utah plus the North Rim of the Grand Canyon. Joan relished hiking with her New Mexico fellow travelers. It was a visit of three weeks which allowed us, with the help of neighbor, Barbara McCormick, to plan an extra adventure: three ladies on a motor trip to El Paso and Ciudad Juarez. In 2005 Joan and I once again crossed the English Channel on the ferry and proceeded to Croatia with British tourists sharing a motor coach with us. It was a fascinating and friendly country that had recovered from the Balkan Wars of 10 years earlier.

Our final trip together, in 2006, would be one of my favorite Grand Circle Travel tours: the Canadian Rockies. Joan and I met our fellow passengers in Seattle and saw more sublimely beautiful scenery. Again, we had pleasant days with our La Vida Llena friends upon our return.

Joan and I enjoyed the times we were able to be together. We like to take walks; we like to play Scrabble; we are both curious about the world around us. She made a difference at the beginning of our friendship and every day since. I am 86 years old and may be giving up extensive travel. She is 82 and dislikes the hassle of present-day airport procedures. We may not be able to travel together again. We will continue our frequent correspondence.

Like other aging people, I am rich in memories. Memories connect us to the precious persons who have entered our lives. There are hundreds of those never-to-be-forgotten individuals. Joan keeps coming into my mind as one who was a part of one happy adventure after another. She was a significant influence in my life.

Putting Stress to Good Use
by
Clare Wilson

Sometimes the job I enjoyed for 11 years was so rewarding that I believed I was overpaid. I was hired as assistant to the manager of a consulting engineering company. The position seemed very challenging from the start and grew more complex as time went on.

When I arrived, the engineering staff represented every discipline and numbered 35, but soon increased to double the size of the company. I arranged board meetings at our office and open houses which included a musical ensemble. These activities were fun. During one of our open house events our switchboard received an incoming call from a voice that announced a bomb threat. My boss, who had had a few cocktails, didn't believe a word of it. However, the vice president of the company evacuated the place and called the police. No bomb was discovered, so the musicians tuned up again as glasses were refilled. Now, how much fun was that! The culprit turned out to be a former employee who had recently been terminated.

I was directed to hire and train new clerical staff as we increased manpower. However, this was an Equal Opportunity Employer

(EOE) I worked for. The new EOE guidelines for hiring employees directed me as follows: I could no longer administer a typing test to determine typing speed, spelling, neatness, accuracy. Nor could I dictate a letter for the applicant to transcribe for mailing. The interviewer had to turn to intuitive skills and draw out the interviewee about job experience and related topics. This DIY (do-it-yourself) system brought to the front office a receptionist with poor typing skills, but a sharp wit. She kept the rest of us happy in our work.

Individual reports from the secretary of each division usually required me to do a few re-reads before merging them into a single volume. These volumes were then shipped via FedEx to our corporate headquarters in Denver. This usually made for a high pressure Friday afternoon. The FedEx guy would wait at the desk glaring at me until I had the project completed and I could give him the "GO" sign.

Each month it became a challenge to be ready on time and I often wondered if there was another, better, less stressful way to use my energy. Perhaps the energy generated during month-end activities could be put to better use; for example, saving a life, taking 911 calls, driving an ambulance, helping to deliver a baby, or learning CPR and being prepared to use it. These ideas kept returning month after month, until my thoughts began to engage my feelings and I recognized most of these options encompassed nursing. When I was a young high school student, nursing had been my first career choice. I wondered if it was too late for me to enter a new field — at age 48 could I still study?

I would have to give up many activities I enjoyed in order to focus on studying. Could I have a social life? Perhaps fellow students could become my support and social group. I would want to continue working, if possible; but only if my spouse could help with cooking and shopping.

When I staggered home one Friday, exhausted and wasted, my husband realized something was different — I appeared exhausted

AND happy. He picked up on my enthusiasm as I described my eagerness to pursue a degree in nursing. He was all for it, including doing the cooking and shopping — and feeding the animals. He suggested that I go ahead and pursue whatever I had in mind.

I approached the University of Albuquerque where I already had taken some general courses, and was accepted without delay. The "new" math worried me, so I registered for that immediately and passed with no problem. At the same time I enrolled in Anatomy and Physiology which I found fascinating. I earned an A for the semester. Being rewarded for studying was great — it was more satisfying than a paycheck.

I was off at a gallop and never happier. Even with my husband behind me all the way and tutoring me in all my science courses, it took me seven years to complete my degree and my age advanced into the next decade. As I charted my patients' notes on a routine Friday and counted my blessings, how could I not look back and wonder who was binding and mailing the monthly report with the FedEx guy glaring at her — or him? It wasn't I.

About the Authors

Gee Arrom, born in 1930, was raised on a small farm and educated in the East. Most of her life was spent raising five children and traveling extensively around the world — living in Alaska, the Virgin Islands, England and Spain, to name a few. She has 20 grandchildren (with two marriages) and seven great-grands. Her later years are spent visiting the kids.

Phyllis Barnes was born in 1937 in Santa Monica, California, but spent most of her youth in Oregon. She has three children and three grandchildren. She retired after 22 years from the Protocol Office at Los Alamos, New Mexico, and moved into La Vida Llena in 2009.

Elizabeth Shellabarger Bayne born in San Diego, California, in 1939, graduated from the University of Colorado-Boulder with a master's degree in Music Education. Elizabeth taught music in public schools and maintains a private voice studio. She has sung in church choirs since age 11, performed in musical theatre and presently sings professionally in Albuquerque. For 28 years she assisted her husband in his registered investment advisory firm. A widow, she moved to La Vida Llena in 2009.

Shirl Brainard retired as a Design & Color Theory instructor from a Michigan community college. She was one founder of a local art gallery that showed her work and taught in community education at the University of New Mexico and other venues. At age 81, she is an active creative participant at La Vida Llena.

Patricia Risley Campbell was born in 1932 in New Jersey and grew up in Missouri. She taught elementary children for 36 years in Peru, New Mexico and Texas. She retired in 2002. In 2008 she moved to La Vida Llena and now enjoys many activities including singing and teaching Spanish.

Louise Chambellan is a Navajo Indian, born at Fort Defiance, Arizona, in 1929. As a child she lived in a hogan and helped her family herd sheep and goats. She left the reservation in 1946 to enter a different world learning about different places and races. She worked for Fred Harvey at Needles, California, married, and continued her education to become a credentialed teacher.

Lillian Chavez was born in northeastern Colorado in 1918. She was introduced to the world of music at an early age and throughout her life she has cherished the gift of love for music which she was given. She is still sharing that gift by performing several concerts a year at La Vida Llena where she resides.

Susan A. Cho is a native southern Californian born in 1943. Professional social work in mental health and Family Practice medical education in Kansas and Arizona was her career for 40 years. Lured by the special light and landscapes of New Mexico she retired and moved to La Vida Llena in 2005. Along with volunteer activities, she continues doing social work part-time.

Barbara Clark was born in Kansas City in 1926. After graduation from the University of Kansas, she married Tom, a West Point graduate. They lived all over the world and took advantage of their many travel opportunities. It was a life she would not trade for anything on earth.

Margo Davis was born and educated in Minnesota from 1923-1949. She was registered as a Public Health Nurse in five states. During her career as a nurse, she primarily served as an appointed and elected community participant in specific health projects. In January 1989 she moved to La Vida Llena.

Hélène "Lanie" Dickel was born (1938) and raised in Massachusetts. She graduated from Mount Holyoke College (B.A.) and University of Michigan (Ph.D.). Lanie was a Research Professor of Astronomy at the University of Illinois for nearly 40 years. After retiring, she moved to La Vida Llena in 2005.

Jean Dilley, born in Cleveland, Ohio, in 1921, graduated from Ohio Wesleyan University in English in 1943. During the war she worked at the Applied Physics Lab of Johns Hopkins University where she met her husband, Neil, who worked for Kodak until he retired. Traveling has been Jean's passion and she has visited and learned about most areas of the world.

Barbara Fentiman was born in Colorado in 1930. She attended Colorado State College of Education, married and worked at the National Bureau of Standards. In 1968 she joined the Central Intelligence Agency where work took her to Asia, Africa and Europe, until retiring in 1986. She now enjoys retirement in New Mexico.

Christiane Fiquet-Bart is a native of France, born in 1926. She had a career as a bilingual secretary, travel agent, and in investment banking and lived in several countries: France, England, Africa, Canada and the USA. Christiane has been practicing Tai Chi for 17 year. She moved from California to La Vida Llena in beautiful New Mexico in 2003.

June Fischer, now at the age of 86, has lived the last four years at La Vida Llena. As a native New Yorker she spent the first 67 years of her life raising a family of four children and having a 20 year career teaching music in the schools. She lived in England for the 14 years prior to moving back to the USA.

Mary Lou Goodwin was born (1927) in Camden, Oklahoma, and attended schools in Tyler, Texas. She graduated from Highland Park High School and Southern Methodist University, Dallas, Texas. She married a Methodist minister, BC Goodwin, and lived in 10 parsonages in three states. They raised four amazing children. Mary Lou moved to La Vida Llena in 2003 from Santa Fe, New Mexico, and was widowed in 2009.

Colleen Hill is a native Californian born in 1928 in Inglewood, California. She married young, had four children, and completed one year of college at Redlands University. She worked in her husband's dental office and had various other jobs, including running a swim school and being a secretary for a blind psychologist. Her physical abilities have been limited by illness since 1968, but her involvement in life around her continues to this day.

Carol Hjellming was born in Iowa in 1938 and grew up in Chicago. She has lived or traveled in most of the USA and 24 other countries. Since moving to La Vida Llena full-time in 2011 she has joined Bib 'N Tucker, heads the Quilts of Valor group, and is a member of the Employee Appreciation Fund committee.

Ollie Mae Hopper was born in Birmingham, Alabama, in 1929. She resided in Knoxville, Tennessee, for 20 years and graduated from the University of Tennessee. She taught art in Oak Ridge, Tennessee, and Albuquerque, New Mexico. She has lived at La Vida Llena for 16 years and has shown art work at four galleries in Santa Fe and 10 in Albuquerque.

Jeannine Hudson-Green resided in New Mexico since 1952. A native of France, she met and married an American GI in Paris at the end of WWII. Despite careers over her lifetime, her passion always centered on home and family. She had just finished her piece for this book when Parkinson's disease finally overtook her.

Mari-Luci Jaramillo, a native New Mexican, was born in 1928. During her career she was a teacher, a professor, a University administrator, and a vice president of a major corporation. She also served as Deputy Assistant Secretary of Defense for Inter-American Affairs in the Pentagon and was the first American women ambassador to Latin America.

Kay Johnson was born in Montreal, Canada, in 1932. As a jeweler/metalsmith, she quickly learned the excitement of study and work throughout western USA. Until retirement in 2006, her tool loaded suitcase was always ready to travel. Teaching, though an on-going facet, never captured her heart as did hands-on metal work.

Dorothy Hendryx Kollman was born on a farm in Iowa in 1926. One year later she moved to the small town of Center Point, Iowa. Her passion for volunteering has lasted for over fifty years. She has resided in La Vida Llena since 2003, where she continues to volunteer.

Dorothy Losee was born in 1923 in Hampton, Iowa. She graduated from University of Iowa where she met her Navy pilot husband. Upon his graduation from law school they moved to Artesia, New Mexico, where they lived for 61 years. She was extremely active in civic and church volunteer work. But her most cherished accomplishment was being a wife and mother.

Virginia "Ginna" Strike Malone was born in 1927, raised in southern California, New Mexico and Texas, graduated from the University of New Mexico, married and raised two children. After the death of her husband, she returned to UNM, got a Ph.D., and became a psychologist, mediator, and trainer. She married again. After his death and her retirement she moved to live another life at La Vida Llena.

Renee Mazon is a native New Yorker born in 1929. She has a happy life in New Mexico with her best friend and her fur-child, Goliath. She spent most of her working life in retailing and retired three times. Renee is an art person and enjoyed making and selling one-of-a-kind jewelry. She collects giraffes.

Josephine D. "Jo" Mechem, born 1926, was educated in the Denver schools. She worked in the insurance industry, fell in love and married Stanley Galloway. They moved to New Mexico and raised four children. Cystic Fibrosis was the highlight of numerous volunteer commitments. For 25 years she played cello in the Santa Fe, Albuquerque Civic and New Mexico symphonies. Jo was widowed in 1972 and married Edwin Mechem in 1976.

Ruth Shore Mondlick (1931) was born and raised in Rhode Island. She married Martin Mondlick, and they moved to Albuquerque, New Mexico, with their two sons in 1964. Ruth taught school for six years. She later earned her Ph.D. at the University of New Mexico and enjoyed a fulfilling career in Psychology.

Jeanne Moore was born in southern California in 1927. Her art studies at the University of Southern California influenced her approach to raising four children. Her full time homemaking and opportunities to serve the Lord gave her a freedom to pursue her desire and need to be creative. As a resident of La Vida Llena she still enjoys watercolor painting and now is also an avid potter.

Irene Myers, age 91, grew up in Philadelphia, Pennsylvania, where she started her 45-year Certified Professional Secretarial career. She married Charles in the military and lived in Japan, Italy and Germany. They had four children; her son currently works at Sandia Labs in Albuquerque. Irene is known as the Flower Lady at La Vida Llena.

Maryann Nordyke was born in 1924 in Indianapolis. She has been an advisor to Psychology graduate students at UCLA, a lecturer and writer on American Decorative Arts at the Los Angeles County Museum of Art, a designer of fine jewelry, a researcher and lecturer on gems and minerals at the Smithsonian Institution. She writes a column, "Know Your Board," at La Vida Llena.

Ann Olander was born in 1919 in Illinois. She graduated with an RN degree in 1939 and became an American Airline stewardess. She was married to a Flight Surgeon for 43 years and had six children. In 1988 Ann received the Humanitarian Award for the Illinois Medical Association. She moved to La Vida Llena in 2006.

Shirley L. Patterson was born in Texas in 1933. Earning a Ph.D. in Social Work at the University of Wisconsin, Madison, she taught for 33 years in graduate schools of Social Work at the University of Kansas and Arizona State University. Prior to her teaching career, she worked in the Topeka, Kansas, inner city and with a War on Poverty program in Kansas City, Kansas. Shirley took up photography in retirement and has taken most and edited all the photos in this book.

Regina Resley was born and raised in central Pennsylvania. She was educated at Penn State and Ohio State in Social Group Work. Married to a West Point graduate, she traveled the world as an Army wife. At age 82 she still volunteers in several organizations and is a puppeteer in elementary schools.

Mary Ansel Roney was born in 1925 in Oklahoma. She moved to Roswell, New Mexico, in 1947 to teach school. She married a native New Mexican, attended Colorado Women's College, Oklahoma University and University of New Mexico. She taught before her marriage and after her children were in college. She moved to La Vida Llena in 2009.

Betty Jo Sargent arrived in this world April 18, 1926, in Wenatchee, Washington. Her early life was spent learning ABC's and swimming in Lake Chelan, Washington. After college Betty Jo's careers were teacher and church musician in the Seattle area, Turkey and Germany. She was a talented painter and illustrator of children's books while retired at La Vida Llena. Betty Jo left this world on December 25, 2011.

Mary Ellen Simms, born in South Dakota in 1935, soon became an "Okie." Educated in Arkansas, she student taught at Little Rock Central High one year prior to the battle for integration. An educator for life, she and her husband retired to La Vida Llena in 2009 to live close to family.

Connie Thompson is a native New Mexican born in 1929. She is a former City Councilor and Mayor of The City of Española, New Mexico. She is the mother of three daughters. She moved to La Vida Llena in 2008 and has become involved in activities offered there.

Mary Ann Wade was born in 1941 in Washington, D.C. She earned a B.S. in Education at Miami University and enjoyed a career as an elementary school teacher, interrupted periodically by motherhood, single parenthood and step-motherhood. When she is not reading to her grandchildren, Mary Ann will be found quilting, writing, drawing, gardening or on photography expeditions with her husband, Campbell.

Constance "Connie" Walker was born in Massachusetts in 1925. Her work experience began with five years in a Detroit pharmaceutical laboratory. After marriage and motherhood, her work life concluded with 17 years as a librarian. Retirement has consisted of 12 years in rural North Carolina and, as a widow, 16 years at La Vida Llena.

Clare Wilson was born in 1931, in Lancaster, Pennsylvania, where she raised kids with emphasis on "Cleanliness is next to Godliness." In 1965 she fled to New Mexico with her children and pets, then changed her career goal to enter nursing and graduated with an associate degree in Nursing (ADN) in 1988.